The Guide to
ODD NEW YORK

Unusual Places, Weird Attractions and the City's Most Curious Sights

First Edition

Allan Ishac and Cari Jackson

Allan Ishac LLC • New York

First Edition published in the United States of America in 2010
by Allan Ishac LLC
24 Fifth Avenue, Suite 1402
New York, NY 10011
info@oddnewyork.com

Copyright ©2010

Cover and Interior Design by Andrea Jennings/MadCreek Design & Creative
Cover and Interior Illustrations by JJ Rudisill

Photo credits: Serge Milman (Joe Ades); Chiaoi Tseng (5 Pointz); Lorcan Otway (Junk Tower)

First Edition
Printed in the United States
EAN 13: 978-0-615-37253-2
ISBN: 0-615-37253-8

Publisher's Note: Neither Allan Ishac LLC nor the authors has any interest, financial or personal, in
the locations listed in this book. While every effort was made to ensure that all data was accurate
at the time of publication, we advise calling ahead or checking websites to confirm details.

Allan's Acknowledgments

Thanks go to my old friend Larry Trepel who keeps me laughing with his double-barreled sense of humor no matter how weird or hard life gets. Helene Silver, my former publisher and friend, generously offered her knowledge of all things literary on this book and steered us wisely as she always does. Andrea DiNoto, our editor, is the consummate pro and helped us get this one right, too. Jason Coustou Garangeat provided research, photography, and writing for some entries. Andrea Jennings, always with a smile and her awesome energy, made these pages look beautiful. And, finally, a big thank you for the perseverance and talent of Cari Jackson.

Cari's Acknowledgments

Thank you to my husband, JJ Rudisill, without whose help, cheerleading and attentive listening, this book would not have been possible. Thank you to my son, who behaved so well while traveling on assignment. Thank you to Yossi Halperin, who conducted research and contributed writing on the Mole People and Freedom Tunnel entry. Thank you to all of my friends who pointed me to new places to visit.

Cari's Dedication
To the most intrepid traveler, Solomon J.
May your life be full of wild adventures and people of great heart.

Allan's Dedication
To everyone who considers themselves odd, strange, offbeat,
unusual, eccentric and weird. Welcome.

Table of Contents

WEIRD FOR A DAY (OR MAYBE A WEEK)

THE ODDER SIDE OF MIDNIGHT

BIZARRE BYGONES

Passing Peculiarities

Introduction

Where has all the weirdness gone? That's a question a lot of New Yorkers and visitors have been asking recently as the city has become more tame and sanitized. While this "cleaning up" of New York has improved our quality of life, it has also marginalized avant-garde elements, fringier folks, quirkier neighborhoods. Many of us who treasured the city's embrace of extremes are bemoaning the loss of a kookier New York.

That offbeat, unconventional side isn't gone. Hidden maybe, under the radar a bit, but it's definitely not dead. And *The Guide to Odd New York* proves it. This book includes the irreverent, the occasional, the unexpected, and the weird. It even pays homage to oddball people, places and things that are gone but not forgotten. It's for locals and adventurous visitors who want to get past the predictable to encounter a more unusual and esoteric New York.

The Guide to Odd New York sends you on the "off-the-tour" tour, pulling back the curtain on a side of the city that's been slowly disappearing. There's the nostalgic Sideshow School and old-time circus freaks in Coney Island, for instance, the magenta haze of Tribeca's psychedelic Dream House, and the kitschy Mermaid Parade. Discover forms of eccentric worship with the Crabapple Chapel and Mummified Mother Cabrini in upper Manhattan. Partial to odd erotica? Don't miss Miss Vera's Finishing School For Boys Who Want To Be Girls or the Troma Studio tour, makers of schlock sex and horror films in Long Island City.

You'll find a surprising or outrageous entry on every page, and we've tossed in a whole lot of photos, too—to feed your insatiable eyeballs. And just to prove that this city remains the place where anything can happen, true New Yorkers share their "Only In New York" tales of surreal, sometimes funny, often shocking moments.

The Guide to Odd New York invites immersion and adventure. Get lost in a place, leave the common footpaths, and enjoy some wonderfully slanted and sensational views of our city.

Allan Ishac
Cari Jackson
New York City, 2010

A reader's note: because this city is in constant flux, call or check websites where applicable for the most current information, directions, and news on these locations. And refer to our geographic index in the back of the book so you can hit three or four spots in a couple hours when you're visiting a particular neighborhood.

Abandoned Subway Tunnel Tour
Down the rabbit hole with the underground Indiana Jones.

Where: Intersection of Court St. and Atlantic Ave.
When: See website for schedule
Phone: 718-941-3160
Getting there: F, G to Bergen St.; A, C, G to Hoyt and Schermerhorn St.
Fee: $15 for adults, $10 for children
Website: brooklynrail.net

Every other Sunday morning, a queue of curiosity seekers stretches along the length of sidewalk outside Trader Joe's at the intersection of Court St. and Atlantic Avenue in Brooklyn. A Jeep blocks traffic in the turn lane, and two burly dudes block the box, standing guard over an open manhole in the middle of the street. A man passes a clipboard down the line. Once he sees that everyone has signed their lives away, he motions for a small group to follow him. These innocents—dressed in street clothes, like they're out for a day of shopping, no tools in hand, no surveyors maps—march in a neat line to the intersection, and disappear, one by one, down the manhole.

Slowly, passersby begin to notice. They stop in the middle of the crosswalk and look back over their shoulders. No, those aren't Con Ed guys. No, they're not from the gas company. "What's going on?" one asks. "We're going into the oldest subway tunnel in the world!" a tour member beams.

Down the rabbit hole the explorers go into the world of Bob Diamond, the rotund Jewish Indiana Jones who discovered the tunnel back in 1979. Disillusioned with his electrical engineering studies at Pratt, Diamond stumbled upon a reference to a mythical tunnel where supposedly John Wilkes Booth's diary was buried and where pirates had hidden their loot. An obsession was born. Diamond pored over historical records and navigated the city's bureaucracy in a quest to find the world's proto-subway. Piecing together clues, he found one manhole cover smaller than any of the others on Atlantic Avenue. Thinking this might be his portal, he gained access to it, crawled through an 18-inch-wide passageway, and then, literally, clawed through the dirt with his hands until he came upon the entrance.

Today Diamond's tourists can climb down a slick ladder through that same opening in the city street and into the same dirt hole—although, fortunately, it's a bit bigger than when he originally staked it. Then it's a slow teeter across a board over a mud puddle, a quick duck under a pipe, and a few steps through a doorway cut through a wall—a portal in time. A makeshift stairway leads to the tunnel floor.

In operation only from 1844 to 1845, the tunnel was finally sealed in 1861. During WWI, our government searched the tunnel for German spies suspected of brewing mustard gas down there. During prohibition, a bootlegger named Cavanaugh used the tunnel as a distillery, as evidenced by labeled bottles found left behind. Other than that, the tunnel fell into obscurity until Bob's big day.

Inside, wheelbarrows filled with old tools and shovels stand along the wall. There's some light from hanging bulbs, but visitors are instructed to bring flashlights to illuminate the path, rutted from buried railroad ties and littered with cobblestones. You can still see the whitewash on the ceiling, which helped brighten the tunnel in its heyday, before electrification.

After a group enters, Bob descends the staircase and starts to regale the curious with tunnel stories. Currently, he's on yet another quest to dig through the underbelly of Atlantic Avenue to access another section of the tunnel, where he believes a train car is buried, perfectly preserved. He has backing from National Geographic and the dig had been planned for spring 2010.

Bob's tenacity and enthusiasm is half the attraction on this tour, as this portly eccentric, with a sly grin, tells tales from his perch on a milk crate. He and the tunnel enjoy a symbiotic relationship; you get the sense that one cannot exist without the other, as if the walls of the underground world would come crashing down if Bob ever walked away from his charge.

Abracadabra
Shock and awe with a pinch of belching powder.

Where: 19 W. 21st St., between 5th and 6th Aves.
When: Monday–Saturday, 11 a.m–7 p.m.; Sunday, 12–5 p.m.
Phone: 212-627-7523
Getting there: F, V to 23rd St.; R, W to 23rd St.
Website: abracadabrasuperstore.com

An eager onlooker stands in the magic section of Abracadabra, a costume and prop shop (nay, institution), watching Cano the Magic Man demonstrate sleight-of-hand with a faux gold coin, when an anxious fellow approaches the counter and inquires about the rental coffin he had ordered. It is January. Halloween is long past. And one wonders whether this guy is simply goferring for a movie production or if he has some necrophilic dungeon freak show planned for later that night. In this shop, the imagination easily runs wild.

For nearly two decades, this Flatiron District emporium has supplied the movie industry, nightclubs, celebrities and regular folks with their sensational prop, costume and funny wig needs. In 2007, brothers Joe and Bob Pinzon took over management. They toned down the staff's notorious surliness, cleared the air of the choking fog of dust and attempted to organize the overwhelming clutter. But Abracadabra still teems with two chaotic floors of novelties like noses, horns and bug-eyed glasses. Towering gargoyles, gory body parts and life-size monsters terrorize the landscape. Row upon row of dramatic masks, wigs and mascot outfits line the walls.

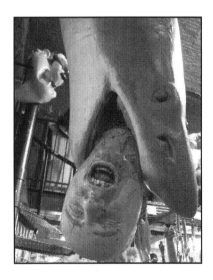

Need a severed finger? Got that. Fart powder? Check. Electric chair complete with convulsing corpse? You bet.

Downstairs, you'll find hundreds of slut-for-a-night, witch, nurse, and pirate ensembles, and behind the counter are even more elaborate costume rentals. Despite the dozens of Halloween décor stores that pop up around the city every September, Abracadabra remains the one essential stop for your year-round masquerading and marauding needs.

Astoria Live Chicken Meat Market

With a chop, chop here and a slice, slice there.

Where: 31-37 20th Ave. at 33rd St., Astoria, Queens
When: 7 days a week, 8 a.m.–6.30 p.m.
Phone: 718-777-7249
Getting there: N, W to Ditmars Boulevard

If you feel queasy at the sight of blood and gore, stay away from the Astoria Live Chicken Meat Market. On the other hand, if you want to have an experience that puts you a million miles from the modern, polished and ultra-cosmopolitan world of midtown Manhattan, then this cackling, quacking, crowing cacophony is for you.

Located only two blocks from the last subway stop in Astoria, the market feels more like it belongs to the sidewalk stalls of a Third World street bazaar than one of the five boroughs. Of course, more than 120 nationalities coexist in Queens with about 138 languages spoken here (in fact, this neighborhood is said to be the most diverse in the world), so it's a place where the unusual is the norm.

The moment you walk through the door of the market you're greeted by the sickly sweet, somewhat overpowering smell of fresh blood. The first large, windowless room you enter is packed with the cages of live chickens, Guinea hens, fowls, pigeons and ducks, all awaiting their fates. Customers handpick the live animal that they want to have slaughtered and butchered right in front of them—a chop fest that is not for the faint-of-heart.

In the back of this warehouse-like space, larger animals are kept. Goats, lambs, and even a calf or two roam a large enclosed area resembling an indoor corral with a floor covered in hay. Next is the slaughter room, where a freshly killed lamb or goat will be hanging upside down, blood draining out, while another is getting skinned.

The meat sold here is 'halal,' which means that the animals are slaughtered following Islamic law. Accordingly, they must be treated gently and killed by hand with a sharp knife using a rapid slicing of the jugular vein while the name of God is evoked. This process theoretically ensures a swift and painless death. It takes about 45 minutes for a calf to be prepared, a half-hour for a goat or lamb, and five minutes for poultry. The butchers and cleaners work swiftly, shuffling the meats away with deft hands and knives as quickly as croupiers handling a stack of chips.

If you're used to buying your meat and poultry plucked, trimmed, skinned, chopped and vacuum-sealed with a kiss before it reaches your grocer's freezer, this butcher shop is a throwback to another era. You'll not only see how your hamburger actually reaches the pillows of your sesame buns, you'll get a glimpse of a time when we ventured into our backyards to catch dinner. And, boy, was it fresh.

Babeland

Sex is not a dirty word.

Where: 94 Rivington St., near Ludlow St. (visit website for other locations)
When: Sunday–Wednesday, 12–10 p.m.; Thursday–Saturday, 12–11 p.m.
Phone: 212-375-1701
Getting there: F, J, M, or Z to Delancey St.
Website: babeland.com

If you're from Amsterdam, turn the page. Babeland will probably seem tame compared to the permissive culture you enjoy.

But if you're visiting New York from a more staid and humorless place, feeling nostalgic for Time Square's peep shows and other seedy adult book stores, Babeland has enough stimulation to keep you fully engaged. Formerly called Toys in Babeland, this sex boutique is especially refreshing to New Yorkers who watched two "shut-em down, clean-em up" Republican administrations turn the X-rated 42nd Street into a Disney theme park.

At first glance, this popular sex shop (with locations around the city) seems mainly to cater to girls looking for plastic boyfriends. But closer inspection reveals an extensive collection of titillating toys for both sexes, including dildos, vibrators, massage accessories, flavored you-name-its, man sleeves, harnesses, and restraints. Almost everything is on display so you can touch it and feel it (warning: if you insert it, you buy it).

Babeland permanently eliminates the need for trench coats, sticky catalogs, P.O. boxes, and user guides in poorly translated Chinese. Every Babeland store has a friendly, enthusiastic and respectful staff imparting useful information about all the pleasure toys on display without a snicker or a blush. Shy about questions? No problem—little info cards appear next to each product so that you can better understand how to use, clean and store your Fleshlight Vulva, rabbit vibrator or leather cock ring. If you'd prefer to inquire about your butt plug with absolute discretion, Babeland also offers an after-hours, private shopping option.

Babeland carries everything that makes for better sex and masturbation, and unlike sleaze dives, the shops are bright, clean and tasteful. The Babeland staff offers well-attended workshops on using their sex toys safely for maximum pleasure, while author and pornographic filmmaker Tristan Taormino gives frequent instruction on her specialty, anal sex. Sex books abound, as well as get-you-in-the-mood games, naughty bedroom dice, and chocolate body paint. The lickable list is endless.

If for no other reason than to subvert the influence of fundamentalist religious groups and hypocritical conservative politicians who try to mandate, legislate and regulate what we can do with our pleasure orifices, pay homage to the resiliency and spunk of Babeland.

Broad Channel
Kind of like a trip to Venice—just bring your own Budweisers.

Where: The hinterland of Queens
When: Always and forever
Getting there: A to Broad Channel (Far Rockaway line)
Website: broadchannelny.com

The locals call this cluster of former summer bungalows, tightly knit along a grid of inland canals, the "Venice of New York." Go ahead, snicker if you want. Just don't do it in front of a Broad Channeler if you're fond of those pearly whites.

This quirky hamlet, just one mile long by a few blocks wide, occupies the only inhabited island in the Jamaica Bay Wildlife Refuge. And just as an estuarial blend of freshwater and saltwater produces its own species of fish and plants, Broad Channel is home to the curious breed of New Yorker you get when you press the borough of Queens against wilderness marshland.

Up until 1982, the city leased the land to the year-round dwellers who, for the most part, made meager livings off the water. Narrow canals divide every street on one side of the island, so that a majority of the homes come with a backyard and a dock. Elsewhere, ramshackle bungalows sit entirely on stilts. The city refused to sell for decades, creating an "Us" against "Them" mentality. But when the city started selling the 25x100 foot waterfront lots to residents for $5,000, "Us" won big time.

Now that longtime locals own the place and are sitting on a real estate gold mine, they are as possessive as feudal lords. When the DOT wanted to put up No Parking signs so that emergency vehicles could access the street, Broad Channel said "Screw that!" The signs mysteriously disappeared. The American Littoral Society, headquartered in Broad Channel, regularly beats down attempts to develop outlying wetlands. And talk about self-protective. One Broad Channeler confessed that he bought the vacated house next door "because I don't want to get stuck with bad neighbors."

Still, Broad Channel has its charms. You'll take the A train from points west in the city, and step off at the Broad Channel stop to marsh grasses brushing your legs. An egret perches in an empty lot, the water laps at pilings, and the streets are all but empty. You will feel conspicuous but not unwelcome. Things to do: Hike the 1.8-mile West Pond Loop, where more than 300 species of migrating birds layover. Charter a boat out of Smitty's Bait and Tackle (718-945-2642). Hit the nostalgic Grassy Point Bar & Grill (718-474-1688) for a beer (not a glass of wine, sissy). View the sunset from a deck over the bay at the Bayview Restaurant (718-634-4555; bcbayview.com).

When you forget where you are (and you will), walk to any dead end on the west side. In the distance, the Manhattan skyline rises up behind Brooklyn, a faraway reminder that you're still in the five boroughs. Broad Channel is a miracle of existence, a bastion of authenticity, a nice place to visit– but they won't let you live there.

Buzz-A-Rama Slot Car Racing Track

Miniature speed demons race through the heart of Brooklyn.

Where: 69 Church Ave., between 14th Ave. and Dahill Rd., Brooklyn
When: Open weekends from approximately 2 p.m.–7 p.m.
Phone: 718-853-1800
Getting there: F to Church Ave.
Fee: Rates are per 15 minutes and vary according to track
Website: Ha! You'll barely get this guy to answer the phone.

While many longtime residents of Brooklyn lament the steady creep of Manhattan (boutiques and wine bars and gastro pubs, oh my!), one little oasis of old-fashioned fun remains: Buzz-A-Rama Slot Car Racing Track. Lured from their Wiis and XBoxes, kids—and adults—tramp in from all over the city for entertainment that features no flashing lights or sound effects, no dancing mascots or rides.

When Buzz Perri opened Buzz-A-Rama in 1965, he competed against as many as forty-five slot car tracks in New York City. Slot cars, which are scale model cars powered by electrified metal strips inside slots that run the length of the track, were an international fad, imported from England via California. Over the years, Buzz followed the trends, adding video games as they showed up on the scene, but maintaining the tracks as his central attraction. By 1979, all of the other tracks in the five boroughs had closed. Today, Buzz-A-Rama is the oldest slot car track in the world still run by its original owner.

Buzz-A-Rama sits on a tacky stretch of Church Avenue in a former supermarket. Teetering stacks of boxes filled with an untold bounty of vintage merchandise line the spare white walls. A glass case holds a sampling of forgotten nutritional supplements, and in the back corner, customers can hit the "fueling center," a selection of vending machines that look like they date from the shop's founding. Yet, the lack of décor doesn't put off the customers, or detract from the visceral excitement of seeing 1/24-scale slot cars fish-tailing around hairpin curves with their characteristic high-pitched whines. Buzz made the wise decision to get American Model Car Raceways tracks, which are sleek, looping modernist masterpieces, in robin's egg blue, black, and bright orange and yellow. He hired a Swede to refinish them in 1990 ("It took him 30 days working 8 a.m. to 4 a.m.," Buzz says), and today they look nearly new.

Open only on weekends, most days the place is packed with birthday parties and regulars. You'll see a gaggle of 8-year-olds lined up next to grown men, who bring Dewalt tool boxes filled with their own prized cars. All stand slack-jawed and transfixed, modulating speed to avoid a wreck. The cars run along a slotted track, but a poorly timed acceleration can send them flying, making for tiny moments of drama. In the back corner, die-hards race on the fastest track, where speeds can reach 100 mph. About a dozen video games still work, but Buzz only turns them on for the birthday parties.

At 74, Buzz still marches about the place, keeping the sugared-up kids in line. His wife, Dolores, works the front counter. Against his accountant's advice, Buzz has no intentions of closing the place. Dolores, a nutritionist, intends for him to live to 140. He still races in the New York City Marathon and looks forward to being the youngest in his age group in the coming year. His passion for slot cars, kids and life will stoke your embers. You'll leave envious of his gene pool and dominion over speed.

Circus Amok
Juggling politics with somersaults of social commentary.

Where: Throughout the five boroughs, see website for schedule
When: Usually throughout September, see website
Fee: Free
Website: circusamok.org

Circus Amok doesn't hide under the protection of a big top. Its entertainers don't adhere to pre-ordained roles, and its subject matter doesn't restrict itself to mainstream interests. This New York City–based circus theater prances through neighborhood squares, throwing up its stage in unexpected places and in a flurry of pandemonium. The band consists of muscular women, the acrobats are lithe men in dresses, and the emcee is an honest-to-God bearded lady. The stilt, juggling and acrobatic acts play not on the theme of childhood mayhem but on social justice. Yet for all the gender bending and political discourse, little kids still take front row.

Circus Amok began staging its wild rumpuses at experimental theaters in 1989. But five years later, it found its true audience not among the avant-garde but with the general public. Circus Amok unleashed its bedlam on public parks and community gardens throughout the city and developed a hodge-podge of enthusiastic fans.

The troupe turns social issues into circus arts, complete with sword juggling and tightrope walking. Incongruous and chaotic, the free shows spark thought along with easy smiles. The 2008 farce titled "Sub-Prime Sublime," for instance, saw a Wizard of Oz plot superimposed over modern-day woes. While the little ones up front cheered the flying somersaults and clowning, the adults attempted to connect the dots between redlining, sub-prime mortgages and the Large Hadron Collider.

The tiny one-ring show travels not from town to town, but from one NYC neighborhood to another—one day at the edges of well-to-do Park Slope, the next on the quad of a housing project in the Bronx. No matter the age or the socioeconomic class of the audience, the pratfalls and the puppets get the point across.

THE TRAPEZE LOFT

Perfect your hula hooping and high flying.

Where: 91 N. First St., between Berry and Wythe Sts., Brooklyn
Phone: 917-415-7544
Getting there: L to Bedford Ave.
Website: thetrapezeloft.com
(check for class schedule)

THE SKY BOX

The ladies work the silks, the cloud swing and the corde lisse.

Where: 342 Maujer St., between Morgan and Waterbury Sts. (in the House of Yes)
Getting there: L to Grand St.
Email: skybox.info@gmail.com
Website: theskybox.org
(check for class schedule)

Over the last decade or so, people started running away with the circus. If you'd like to tell mainstream America to "suck it" and run away yourself, New York City provides two excellent schools for circus arts.

The Trapeze Loft, founded by Tanya Gagné in 1999, offers classes in aerial skills, such as the cloud swing (one big loop of rope), static trapeze, silks and corde lisse (a single hanging rope). Students can also learn tightwire walking, partner acrobatics, contortion, handstands, hula hooping and foot juggling.

The Sky Box is a dedicated practice and performing space, boasting 30-foot ceilings. Jordann Baker opened the Sky Box, while Anya Sapozhnikova founded the all-female troupe Lady Circus, which performs in-house and throughout the city. Classes and workshops include ballet, cloud swing, static trapeze, silks, lyra (an aerial hoop), and pole dancing (the Chinese acrobat type, not the stripper type). The Sky Box's lush, day-dreamy productions combine storylines with live music, imaginative sets, and jaw-dropping aerial stunts. Twice monthly, you can see Karnival of Kuriosities, another high-flying burlesque show. (See also, House of Yes, page 137.)

City Hall Subway Station
A little bit of mischief at the end of the Lexington line.

Where: At the end of the downtown 6
When: Anytime
Website: mta.info/mta/museum
Check website for sanctioned tours

Too few simple thrills exist in the world today, the kind of thrills that make you giddy but not petrified. The kind that might get you scolded but not sued, arrested or shot at. Catching a glimpse of the old City Hall Station on the 6 train is one such thrill, just naughty enough to conjure some giggles and conspiratorial glances as you take the secret loop from the downtown to the uptown tracks.

City Hall Subway Station opened to passengers in 1904, the belle of the Interborough Rapid Transit (IRT) subway system. Adorned with a vaulted Guastavino-tiled ceiling, leaded glass skylights, and chandeliers, the station occupies 400 feet of an elegant loop at the end of the Lexington Avenue line. Like many beauties, the station's heyday was short-lived: her curve and architecture proved impractical as the train system changed to accommodate more traffic. In 1945, a peak year for the rest of the system, City Hall station saw just 600 passengers a day. The entrances were sealed, the glowing skylights covered, her jubilant presence enjoyed no more. She became a ghost, whispered about in subway lore.

While the station has been abandoned, the track has not. At Brooklyn Bridge, ask a conductor if you can stay on the train (or don't, although they'd like you better if you did) and press your face against the windows on the right side. Every 6 train terminating at Brooklyn Bridge takes a sharp right as it exits the downtown track. Just 600 feet along the track, the cars begin a long curve to the left and the old City Hall Station is revealed. Arch after tiled arch floats by—there go the glass tile nameplates in glimmering blue, teal and sienna. The stairway ascends to a mezzanine just out of sight. At the end of the station, the local tracks descend and duck under the express tracks. Then they rise to meet the uptown tracks and run back into Brooklyn Bridge station.

The Transit Museum operates tours through the station on occasion and the only way to get there is by subway. Visitors exit through one door, where the arched platform comes close enough to the train to step off. From the platform, you can marvel at the cathedral of glass above. This is a cool urban adventure that's definitely worth your time, and if you're not into spelunking through the Freedom Tunnel (see page 71), it might be more your speed.

City Island

A mash-up of Newport and The Bronx.

Where: Located just beyond Pelham Bay Park in the Bronx
Getting there: 6 to Pelham Bay Station; Bus #29
to City Island Ave. at Fordham St.
Website: cityisland.com

Take Nantucket, sprinkle in a few cast members from *The Warriors*, slap a Bronx accent on all residents—*voilá*, you've got City Island. This idyllic island sits off the wooly shoulder of The Bronx, where the Long Island Sound meets the East River. And from every socioeconomic class and corner of the Tri-state area, they come—whether for the yacht clubs, the fried fare, the views or the surreal scene.

Surrounded by Pelham Bay to the north, the western edge of Long Island Sound to the east and south, and Eastchester Bay to the west, City Island has always earned its living from the water. From the early 1800s, industry has included a salt works, oyster fisheries, shipbuilding and sail making. Today, the aquatic theme continues. Visitors can rent a little motorboat and fishing tackle for the day from Jack's Bait and Tackle (718-885-2042; jacksbaitandtackle.com). They can enjoy sailing lessons at the New York Sailing Center and Yacht Club (718-885-0335; startsailing.com) or sign up for SCUBA diving lessons at Captain Mike's Diving Services (718-885-1588; captainmikesdiving.com). It's possible to browse antique stores for boating memorabilia or art galleries for nautical-inspired items. And everyone eats the fried anything that comes out of the water at a long row of seafood restaurants on the main drag.

The City Island Nautical Museum (718-885-0008; cityislandmuseum.org), run entirely by volunteers and open only on weekends, tells the island's tale, and these are historically rich waters. Execution Rocks Lighthouse (rumored to derive its names from the British practice of chaining prisoners to the rocks at low tide, and then leaving them to drown) safeguards the waters to the east. From Pelham Cemetery, the only waterfront cemetery in the city, one can view Hart Island also to the east. This is where New York City's unclaimed dead are buried in stacked pine boxes in mass graves by prison inmates. Of the 2,000 burials that take place on Hart Island every year, as many as half are children under 5, making it, quite possibly, the saddest place in America. Yet, the melancholy of Hart Island scarcely seems to affect the summertime-party vibe of its neighbor.

While delicious fare can be found at the City Island Lobster House (718-885-1459; cilobsterhouse.com) or Sammy's Fish Box (718-885-0920; sammysfishbox.com), Johnny's Reef Restaurant (718-885-2086) can't be beat for its homemade tartar sauce, the view and the eclectic scene. Order up some greasy fish fry and a pina colada, and then snag a blue picnic table overlooking the Sound. Tankers, speedboats and sailboats crisscross the water, with Stepping Stone Lighthouse and Long Island in the distance. Kawasakis rev in the parking lot and lovers lean into each other at the water's edge, while children toss French fries to swooping, squealing seagulls. Neither New York nor New England, this nether world offers landlubbers an escape and a salty taste of another era.

Passing Peculiarity

BERLIN WALL

WHERE: 53RD ST., BETWEEN MADISON AND FIFTH AVES.

In a tiny courtyard at the base of an office building, office workers take smoke breaks at café tables. They stare into space or down at their shoes or at their glowing ember. Yet right in front of their faces stands a remnant of the physical space where freedom met oppression: a segment of the Berlin Wall. Crude, bold and abstract graffiti covers five segments of the wall by artists Thierry Noir and Kiddy Citny. On the back, you'll see what appear to be bullet holes. Three other pieces of the wall can be found at the entrance to the Intrepid Sea-Air-Space Museum, in the (temporarily closed) gardens at the UN, and in Battery Park.

City Reliquary Museum
The soul of the city, one rusted relic at a time.

Where: Museum at 370 Metropolitan Ave., near Havemeyer St.;
Window at 307 Grand St. at Havemeyer St., Williamsburg, Brooklyn
When: Open weekends, 12–6 p.m.; Thursdays, 7–10 p.m.
Phone: 718-782-4842
Getting there: L to Bedford Ave.
Website: cityreliquary.org

At the corner of Havemeyer and Grand Streets in Williamsburg, Brooklyn, passersby can peer into a window and see the soul of New York City. Broken pieces of bridges and landmark buildings, odd ephemera picked up from Dead Horse Bay, ancient subway tokens and obsolete road signs fill the City Reliquary storefront and, piece-by-piece, they tell the story of New York.

Brooklyn resident Dave Herman collected the items over many years and displayed them in the storefront window (and just the window) on the ground floor of his building, with permission from his landlord. Passersby could press a button and Herman's recorded voice would lead them on an inside-the-glass-case tour. He also painted directions to nearby landmarks on the brick wall outside, places like the Williamsburg Bridge and McCarren Park, as a service to the crowds that flocked to the hipster nabe. As interest grew, so did his collection.

In 2006, his City Reliquary Museum moved to its current location. The not-for-profit museum hosts block parties, backyard concerts and film nights throughout the year. It also holds programs for kids and directs the annual Miss G Train Pageant. Thankfully, Herman still maintains the original window a few blocks away. Its presence, a backdrop for neighbors coming and going from work, reminds us that life reveals itself in what's left behind.

Coffee Bark

Runaway dogs and torn knee ligaments in Prospect Park.

Where: Prospect Park, Brooklyn, on Long Meadow near the Picnic House
When: Prospect Park daily off-leash hours, 9 p.m.–9 a.m.;
Coffee Bark takes place the first Saturday morning of every month
Getting there: F to 15th St./Prospect Park
Website: fido.org

Coffee Bark is canine chaos. The first Saturday morning of every month it turns parts of Prospect Park in Brooklyn into a slobber fest—an unruly mass of unfettered dogs and free-spirited owners that make you wonder how the city even permits this raucous, ruff-housing event.

Serious dog owners, an odd breed in themselves, provide stellar material for people watching. Add in the stout terriers and uncoordinated mastiffs recklessly knocking everything and everyone out of their way, and you're privy to a few hours of pooch pandemonium that leaves you agog.

There are a few tales of owners who were upended by roiling packs of hounds and left the field with arms broken and ACLs torn. Yet, incredibly, they return to the park the next day smiling, arms in slings, while their dogs careen by with tongues trailing, ears flapping and hump reflexes at the ready.

Coffee Bark bears witness to the genuine joy that dogs and their "people" get from unleashed freedom—in fact, you can hear the ruckus from hundreds of yards away. FIDO, the off-leash advocacy group that sponsors this free-for-all of Milkbones (for the mutts) and free coffee (for the collar clutchers) has a website to keep you posted on the park's dog-related events.

Many park passersby seem to begrudge dogs their off-leash independence, and tension between dog-matic owners and dog-haters exists. But for non-Grinches, a trip to the meadows during Coffee Bark, or during any of the 9 p.m. to 9 a.m. offleash hours in many NYC parks, is a unique experience. Just keep your knees loose and an eye out, and if you bring a dog, make sure you pick up its crap, for crying out loud!

Coney Island Circus Sideshow School
Excuse me, is that a nail sticking out of your cheek?

Where: 1208 Surf Ave. at 12th St.
When: Class schedule varies (check website); Also check website for schedule of Sideshow performances
Phone: 718-372-5159
Getting there: D, Q, N or F to Stillwell Ave.
Fee: From $5 for performances; Class fees vary (check website)
Website: coneyisland.com

The next time someone calls you a freak, do something about it. No, not by rolling your eyelids inside out or head butting the offender with your steel reinforced skull. You'll do better capitalizing on your freakishness by signing up for a class at the Coney Island Circus Sideshow School. This is the site of America's last 10-in-1 sideshow, a professional training school that is serious about your potential talent for gulping blades, seducing snakes, gargling fire, or stopping mousetraps with your tongue.

Homework at the sideshow isn't like that at your normal high school. At a recent class, several students discussed the previous week's assignment with instructor Adam Rinn. "I can only get a really thin nail up my nose," lamented one 20-something investment banker. "Don't worry, your nose will adjust to the width of the nail," Rinn reassured her.

A bartender (a healthier looking version of Amy Winehouse) described how she slid a coat hanger down her throat "to here" and pointed just above her collarbone. "That's great!" Rinn said, clearly impressed, for these skills are no small feat. They require a willingness to set personal safety aside, to eschew all manner of good advice and to perform stunts that discomfort audiences who've been hooked on CSI for years.

The consequences of such a foray into life's margins were expressed by the only young man

in the class: "My Spanish mother saw me pushing the nail up my nose and got hysterical. She called all of our relatives, who then started calling to figure out what was wrong with me." During the class, students learn skills like lying on a bed of nails, sticking their hands in rusty rabbit snares and putting their tongues in mousetraps. They do things with flames that seem foolhardy at best, perilous at worst. There is a science to executing these stunts without causing permanent injury, but the truth is they do hurt and, in fact, can cause permanent injury, as was the case when sideshow emcee Donny Vomit cracked a tooth and snipped off the end of his tongue while performing the mousetrap trick on stage. It certainly leads one to ask, what is wrong with these people?

Those in the class can tell you, there is a *joie de vivre* in the art, showmanship and sacrifice of the sideshow. It evokes a time when simple entertainment required live performers interacting with an audience, as opposed to digital characters interfacing with an avatar. Much of our beloved Coney Island has been dismantled, and the land braces for an uncertain future. But the group Coney Island USA—instigator of the Mermaid Parade and Burlesque at the Beach—long ago recognized the value in America's baser arts and bought its home on Surf Avenue.

So those brave enough will long be able to find escape from the mundane by driving 3-inch nails into tender orifices. And while you may find no deep meaning in placing a flaming stick in your mouth, at least at the Coney Island Sideshow School it's real. You will actually feel the heat on your lips—and if you accidentally breathe in, it could kill you.

Crabapple Chapel

Kooky, handmade backyard shrine to St. Francis.

Where: 116th St., between First and Second Aves. (e-mail for exact address)
When: By appointment only; email LuLu LoLo, lululolo@rcn.com
Getting there: 6 to 116th St.
Fee: Free

To many a tourist's surprise, backyards do exist in New York. These coveted spaces provide refuge from millions of scrutinizing eyes, the racket of road rage and littered sidewalks. They house birdbaths, flower and vegetable gardens, vineyards and pools. And in one particular plot of land, a handmade chapel.

When performance artist LuLu LoLo and artist and playwright Dan Evans moved into their home in East Harlem in 1974, they recognized their embarrassment of riches—a 20 x 30 foot bounty of backyard. That spring, Dan and his friend Tom Yeomans decided they would use the space to pay homage to their spiritual hero, St. Francis of Assisi. The nature-loving, patron saint of living things is said to have once spoken to an almond tree that responded by spontaneously bursting into bloom. Disappointed to learn that almond trees can't grow in New York, Dan and Tom planted a crabapple sapling in Dan's empty backyard instead.

Fast forward to 2005. The little tree grew to a height of 40 feet, nearly to the top of LuLu and Dan's four-story brownstone. That's when Tom and Dan started fantasizing about building a little hut in the shade of the crabapple, similar to the one St. Francis had built in Italy. Dan envisioned something made of twigs that he could meditate in, but Tom's son Ben knew a thing or two about timber framing and hatched a somewhat grander plan. And, so, a little gothic chapel was born in upper Manhattan, with room for two, held together only by wooden pegs. The wood was locally harvested and handpicked, and though humble in size and ingredients, the Crabapple Chapel was awesome in effect.

When asked why he has such a deep reverence for St. Francis, Dan says, "I love his humility. I love how he lets everyone be who they are," as if speaking of a living friend. The chapel achieves this sense of humility. When you walk through the arched doorway, you experience an urge to bow, to kneel, to sit in silence. The deep scent of raw timber fills your lungs, pulling you out of East Harlem and into the middle of a forest. On ledges and in corners, visiting friends and artists have left figurines of birds and squirrels, a cardboard rendition of St. Francis, a manger scene with Igor the Hunchback and photos of deceased pets. It's an odd, but touching tribute to the human-animal connection.

LuLu and Dan, true New York eccentrics, welcome strangers into their home to share this sacred ground. Maybe they realize just how much they have, compared to others who view quiet green space longingly from soot-mottled apartment windows or elevated portions of the subway. In any case, if you want a one-of-a-kind New York experience, let LuLu and Dan know you're on the way.

Passing Peculiarity

BEST BAZONGAS

WHERE: ROBERT F. WAGNER PARK IN LOWER MANHATTAN NEAR BATTERY PARK.

Erotic statues and pervy art installations are easy to find in New York. A particular favorite resides in Robert F. Wagner Park in southern Manhattan. It's the Louise Bourgeois sculpture of two large eyeballs staring out at the Statue of Liberty. Eyeballs? If you see anything other than a pair of giant hooters with stand-up metal nipples, you're neutered. Breast cancer awareness group Babes for Boobs actually used the sculpture in a photo shoot.

De La Vega Museum

One man's vision achieved in a museum to himself.

Where: 102 St. Mark's Pl., near 1st Ave.
When: Monday–Sunday, 1–6 p.m., closed Wednesdays and rainy days
Phone: 212-876-8649
Getting there: 6 to Astor Pl.
Website: delavegamuseum.blogspot.com

James De La Vega, owner of the De La Vega Museum, possesses an outsized ego. This explains how he came to open a museum—more a commercial venture—dedicated to himself.

In the front window, pedestrians glimpse the artist's subversive work "Jesus as a Pedophile," a crude drawing of Jesus with a young boy kneeling before him, along with empty chairs sitting out front labeled "Fat Girls Only" and "Jews Only." Hanging in the storefront, from the walls and from the ceiling, you'll find his magic marker drawings of his mom as Martin Luther King Jr., his mom as Castro, his mom as Mohamed Ali. Look up and there's Dora, the Explorer, about to lick Elmo's butthole. And, then, on the shelves and the racks, you'll find t-shirts, cards and tote bags emblazoned with De La Vega's catchphrase "Become Your Dream" and other inspirational witticisms. How he reconciles these contradictory messages remains a mystery.

A former graffiti artist known for chalking provocative sayings on city sidewalks, De La Vega's life has already been well documented in articles in the New York *Times*, Salon.com, even the *Smithsonian*. He grew up in Spanish Harlem and attended Cornell University, although he claims on his blog that he attended the Sorbonne and Oxford. He further states that he is "recognized internationally as the most important philosopher of this generation." He has been arrested multiple times for painting on public and private property. His most recent arrest in 2004 inspired supporters to attend court proceedings in Free De La Vega t-shirts. In another stroke of bravado, he has run for the New York state senate.

Some might call him full of shit, but at least the brazen De La Vega is honest about the capitalistic path he's taken for his art. His whimsy can redirect a bad mood, as can his evident love for his Mom. He sits out front most sunny days in a hat and mirrored glasses, smoking a cigar. You could ask him what it all means, but you would be missing the point. After all, didn't he just tell you?

The Dream House

Psychedelic Tribeca sound and light experience.

Where: 275 Church St., 3rd Fl., between Franklin and White Sts.
When: Thursdays and Saturdays from 2 p.m. to midnight,
September through June
Phone: 212-925-8270
Getting there: 1 to Franklin St.; A, E, N, R, 6 to Canal St.
Fee: $4 suggested donation
Website: melafoundation.org

There are no neutral reactions to the Dream House. After twenty minutes in this radical sound and light environment, you're either marveling at the eccentricity of artists or you're muttering to yourself, "Get me the hell out of here!"

A collaboration between composer La Monte Young (considered by many to be the granddaddy of minimalist music) and visual artist Marian Zazeela, this provocative installation has been rattling the foundations of a Tribeca brownstone since 1993. As you leave the street and ascend the stairs to the 3rd-floor loft, a sustained, industrial hum grows louder with each step, a bit like approaching the massive turbine room of a thrumming power station.

Entering the moodily lit, modest space, you're enveloped by loud, continuous waves of high and low sine-tone frequencies that ricochet through your chest and invade your brain. Young was inspired to create his complex, synthesized music from sounds he heard as a child—the hum of insects, the whir of car engines, wind howling through telephone wires, train whistles, and even canyon silences. These background sounds were constants in his life and so his music is similarly sustained, overlapping, without beginning or end, ever present and everlasting. The throbbing harmonics are supported by Zazeela's abstract, magenta-colored light installation, sending every sense organ into overdrive.

The official 107-word title of the musical composition you are hearing reads as follows: "The Base 9:7:4 Symmetry in Prime Time When Centered Above and Below The Lowest Term Primes in The Range 288 to 224 with The Addition of 279 and 261 in Which The Half of The Symmetric Division Mapped Above and Including 288 Consists of The Powers of 2 Multiplied by The Primes..." And so it goes for another 68 words, but you get the point—this is a surreal sort of aural adventure.

Four of Zazeela's crescent-shaped mobiles hang from the ceiling casting red and blue shadows on the walls, turning ever so slightly as visitors pass slowly through the room. Spectators often shuffle, crawl, even roll about on the lushly carpeted floor. These slight movements seem to change the sound frequencies dramatically—you can pull a massive head rush with an infinitesimal tilt to the left or right.

The Dream House tempts some visitors to arrive in altered states to prepare the way to nirvana. But the payoffs seem greater when you're fully alert, breathing in the aroma of light incense, staring out the rose-tinted windows to the traffic below, paying close attention to your bodily sensations and reactions. Young has said that the twelve-tone harmonic technique he employs at the Dream House reveals magical frequencies never before heard by the human ear. It's a claim that seems completely plausible as his droning music engulfs you, threatening to pulverize gray matter.

Economy Candy

A massive sugar rush, the old fashioned way.

Where: 108 Rivington St., between Essex and Ludlow Sts.
When: Sunday–Friday, 9 a.m.–6 p.m., Saturday, 10 a.m.–5 p.m.
Phone: 800-352-4544
Getting there: F, V to Second Ave.
Website: economycandy.com

The Economy Candy storefront looms before you, just as it has for nearly 80 years. Your grin widens at the sight of Chiclets, Dots, Clark Bars, Gobstoppers, Jawbreakers, Runts, and Jujyfruits, all stacked neatly in the window, an orderly riot of pastels and primaries. The welcoming embrace of the Economy Candy Kid, the candied charisma of glucose abundance, the innocent appeal of an impending sugar rush—these things dance like syrupy spirits before you...and you haven't even opened the door!

Inside, ohhh, inside are stacks upon stacks of every candy that you ever craved, whether you came of age during the reign of Fun Dip and Big League Chew or Sugar Daddies and Abba-Zabas. Throwback candy cigarettes (now called "candy sticks") brazenly cascade off a display. Behind the glass, halvah and chocolate bon-bons beckon while gigantic lollipops swirl above your head. Jelly beans, MalloBars, PopDrops, Turkish Delights...here, everyone finds an old friend.

35

This iconic establishment opened in 1937 as a corner candy store, featuring barrels of Bit-O-Honey's and heart-shaped boxes of chocolates. Heavy on the gullet, but light on the wallet, every candy has always come at a discount. Over the years, the shop has adapted to heightened health awareness offering sugar-free and low-calorie sweets.They even sell online.

Walk out with a few Reese's Big Cups, two Giant Chewy Sweet Tarts, and a Nerds Rope, a Holy Grail of confection that marries red licorice with a sour pucker. Studies show that too many choices can lead to dissatisfaction with a purchase. The exception proves the rule.

Edgar Allan Poe Cottage

The bizarre life of a master of the macabre, showcased in the Bronx.

Where: 2640 Grand Concourse at East Kingsbridge Rd. and Grand Concourse, Bronx
When: Saturday, 10 a.m.–4 p.m.; Sunday, 1–5 p.m.;
Monday–Friday, 9 a.m.–5 p.m.
Phone: 718-881-8900
Getting there: B, D to Kingsbridge Rd.
Fee: $5
Website: bronxhistoricalsociety.org
Note: Check website for updated information about ongoing restoration.

Several connoisseurs of the peculiar recommended that the Edgar Allan Poe Cottage be included in this book. When Imad Khachan, of the Chess Forum (see page 105), exuberantly listed it first among all the strange places to visit in New York City, it was decided.

Poe, with his tragic life story and macabre literary style, exists both within the canon of detective fiction and at the center of a cult-like following. Few literary giants wield such cross-cultural appeal. Fans travel from around the world to stand in this humble space where Poe began a decline into madness.

The cottage sits just 450 feet north of its original location, in the center of a green space but shadowed by Art Deco high-rises just off the Grand Concourse. In 1846, Poe, his tubercular wife Virginia and her mother retreated to this country cottage hoping, in vain as it turned out, that the bucolic setting would cure his wife's illness. Here, he wrote "The Bells," likely inspired by the carillon at nearby St. John's College, which would become Fordham University. He also penned "Annabel Lee," about his wife's painful death in 1847. Two years later, Poe died under mysterious circumstances, some say while on a bender, in Baltimore.

The cottage holds two authentic relics: Poe's rocking chair and the bed in which his wife died. Other items have been arranged to give the sense that the poet has just stepped out. A planned restoration of the cottage will include a visitor's center, with a swooping roof to resemble a raven.

Enchantments, Inc.
Peddling the magic of witchcraft.

Where: 424 East 9th St., near 1st Ave.
When: Monday, Wednesday–Sunday, 1–9 p.m.; Closed Tuesdays
Phone: 212-228-4394
Getting there: 6 to Astor Pl., L to 1st Ave.
Website: enchantmentsincnyc.com

The arcane, sometimes secretive world of witchcraft has been associated with heresy, paganism and devil worship. It has spawned periods in history replete with witch hunts, religious hysteria, and mob lynchings. Punishments for those even remotely suspected of the craft were brutal. Even mere sympathizers could be subjected to trials by fire, boiling in water and other creative acts of torture. No wonder then, after being forced to survive in the shadows for centuries, practitioners of witchcraft still keep their world hidden from the public eye.

Enchantments, the city's oldest and largest witchcraft and goddess supply store, is an exception. Established in 1982, the store conducts business openly and in the relative safety of New York City's legendary tolerance. Enchantments displays an impressive line of products celebrating witchcraft, pagan worship and magical spells. You will also find all the magical tools you could possibly need for an occult session or wicca gathering in the grove—including athames (a ceremonial, double-edged dagger), chalices, altar pentacles, bells, swords, brooms, skull and gender candles, salt and water bowls, god and goddess statues, cauldrons or libation bowls and wands. A full wall is dedicated to a myriad of magical herbs, everything from

Adam and Eve root to Deer's tongue, Dragon's blood chunks to poisonous Tonka beans (the black, wrinkled legume contains coumarin, which is lethal in large doses). Several warnings not to ingest the herbs are on display but, honestly, who in their right mind would blithely nibble on "Devil's Shoestring?"

One could argue that the best part of being a witch is the ability to effectively cast spells to accomplish magical goals (see Glenda, Medea, Hermoine Granger). For that purpose, you may want to pick up one of Enchantments many hand-blended, essential oil mixtures pulled from the "Witch's Formulary," part of the original Book of Shadows. These oils can be applied as perfumes or used to anoint candles for invoking spirits, attracting love and money, removing evil forces and hexes, or finding a great apartment (this being New York, the oils are often out of stock).

Feeling love lost? Try a bottle of "Come-To-Me," described as a potent oil for increasing sexual magnetism, but carrying the warning "Use With Caution." Can one be too magnetic?

Have you forgotten the exact wording of that "Psychic Self Defense" spell? No worries, you will probably find it in one of the many available books ranging in subject from traditionalist wiccan to ceremonial "magick."

At least one floor assistant at Enchantments, who looked as if he had not seen sunlight in years, was a font of information about witchcraft. Good thing, because everything in the store evokes questions.

Passing Peculiarity

BEST PUBLIC PENIS

WHERE: LOBBY OF TIME WARNER CENTER, COLUMBUS CIRCLE

Perhaps the single best example of public art with a kinky twist is Fernando Botero's bronze Adam and Eve statues in the Time Warner center. They stand 20-feet tall and stark naked with absurd proportions in the exaggerated Botero style. Photo albums worldwide must be filled with shots of tourists stroking Adam's perky manhood — it's burnished clean from daily "hand" jobs.

Enrico Caruso Museum
An operatic obsession hits a high note.

Where: 1942 E.19th St., between S and T Aves., Brooklyn
When: By appointment only
Phone: 718-368-3993
Getting there: B,Q to Kings Highway
Fee: Free
Website: enricocarusomuseum.com

Because passion is infectious, a trip to the Enrico Caruso Museum can convert a feigned interest in opera into true appreciation. To get there, you travel not to the Museum Mile but into the authentic heart of Brooklyn, down a tree-lined street in a deeply Italian neighborhood to the humble home of Aldo Mancusi—also the home of all things Caruso.

Aldo Mancusi's fervor for Caruso, "the best tenor of all time" (this is not debatable), led him on a lifelong quest to acquire anything attached to the man, from his cigarettes to his death mask. Today, costumes, records, photos and even neckties fill all five rooms, plus the hallway and the bathroom of the top floor of Mancusi's Bensonhurst home. Three or four times a month he welcomes the public for a two-hour presentation and a tour. Programs sometimes include opera singers and antipasto, as well as home movies of Caruso. Aldo's perfectly coifed wife, Lisa, greets you at the top of the stairs as though you were headed to a cocktail party. The two snipe at each other as elderly couples who have been together since high school do. When Aldo meanders off topic, Lisa snaps, "Aldo! Back to the point!" It all feels a little like having someone's grandfather pull you aside at a party to show off his collection of model planes or military medals, his wife having heard it all a thousand times before.

Mancusi's collection includes the jewelry of Caruso's mistress, original recordings, and caricatures Caruso drew for an Italian-American newspaper. As Mancusi describes Caruso's bon vivant lifestyle, one begins to understand what opera meant for Italians, who at the turn of the 19th Century were seen by many as dirty garlic eaters threatening the American way of life. During this period, Caruso fetched $15,000 per performance and became the first opera superstar. The Metropolitan Opera, surprised by Caruso's draw, began presenting only Italian, rather than German, operas. Italian boys practiced their crooning the way young black boys practice their jump shots, fingers crossed that a hidden gift would lift them from poverty. Mancusi's mother sang arias and his father, an opera lover, vetted all of his children for musical talent. What the young Mancusi lacked in aptitude, he made up for with enthusiasm.

Alongside his Caruso memorabilia, Mancusi displays his other obsession: old Edison technology, including music boxes, cylinders and gramophones, on which he plays original Caruso recordings. An ordnance technical intelligence specialist during the Korean War, Mancusi can restore nearly any old machine. His prized possession, viewable on private tours, is a Weber DuoArt Player Piano from 1927, which plays scrolls recorded by the legendary George Gershwin. "My mechanical ability allows me to stay in the era in which I want to stay," says Mancusi.

The city has long promised him a home for the museum, but as the years pass, his chances grow slim. No matter. Here, one man's history is best appreciated within the context of another man's home—a life of passion, romance and tragedy tidily organized and idealized by a retired businessman with a penchant for the finer things in life.

The Evolution Store
Dinosaur dung and freeze-dried mice.

Where: 120 Spring St., between Greene and Mercer Sts.
When: Daily, 7 a.m.–7 p.m.
Phone: 212-343-1114
Getting there: 6 to Spring St.
Website: theevolutionstore.com

The interior of The Evolution Store feels like the study of some Victorian-era paleontologist or biologist. Mounted butterflies, beetles, wasps and dragonflies line the walls, alongside primate skulls and branch coral. The glass cases enclose meteorites, trilobite fossils and ammonite fossils that date back hundreds of millions of years. One can also find dinosaur poop, teeth and claws. Taxidermied birds, bats, and monkeys as well as freeze-dried mice stare blankly from all corners. A large case houses actual human skeletons of a girl, a boy, a man and a woman, who carries a fetal skeleton hovering above her pelvis.

The Evolution Store maintains that it procures its skulls, skeletons, hides and insects from a variety of lawful sources. A cane toad plague in Australia led to the abundance of toad pocket purses they carry. The mink, beaver, and coyote skulls—and probably the large selection of penile bones—are by-products of the fur industry. Mounted antelope heads come from legal hunts on game preserves in South Africa. China supplies many of their specimens, such as the delicate and somehow charming bat skeletons, just as it delivers most of the wares for biological supply companies.

For those attracted to the aesthetic of fauna frozen in time, but are unnerved by the methods of procurement, turn to the spectacular bird-wing butterfly, with a life-span of one year and wing span of about 11 inches. Farmers in Peru and New Guinea have to preserve habitat in order to raise this rare and protected species. Most of the common butterflies you see mounted for sale meet their demise in gas chambers, but the bird-wing, by law, must die naturally. They come in vivid colors—green, yellow, blue or orange. You can buy one mounted in a shadow-box frame, and contemplate what its life was like during that one brief but glorious summer.

MAXILLA & MANDIBLE
Your bone-and-bug emporium.

Where: 451 Columbus Ave., between 81st and 82nd Sts.
When: Monday–Saturday, 11 a.m.–7 p.m.; Sunday, 1–5 p.m.
Phone: 212-724-6173
Getting there: B, C to 81st St./ Natural History Museum; 1 to 79th St.
Website: maxillaandmandible.com

Located just off the shoulder of the Natural History museum, this little shop of horrors is named for the two bones of the face responsible for yapping. Appropriately enough, Maxilla & Mandible offers plenty of conversation starters. This nature science emporium specializes in bones—it claims to be the world's first and only osteological store—but also carries bugs, fossils and shells.

Maxilla & Mandible also runs programs for reintroduction of native species of bugs back into the wild and has funded biodiversity projects. Its staff of scientists consults on private and institutional collections. So as you can see, the shop is just the public face of a vast organization of labs, workshops and art studios. May this treasure trove survive as long as its Paleolithic wares.

ONLY IN
NEW YORK
STORIES 1

WALKING BEHIND TWO GIRLS IN UNION SQ.
PARK, I SAW A BIG RAT DART OUT FROM
THE BUSHES. OBLIVIOUS, ONE OF THE GIRLS
STEPPED FLUSH ACROSS THE RAT'S BACK AS IT
CROSSED HER PATH. SHE SCREAMED AND
JUMPED. THE RAT NEVER STOPPED MOVING.

— LARRY TREPEL

One chilly winter twilight night along West 4th Street I saw a prodigious St. Bernard dog deposit an equally prodigious pile of poop in the snow along the curb. The dog and his owner walked off, but almost immediately the door to an apartment along the block opened and an attractive woman dressed just in PJ's and a robe rushed out and placed a thick, lighted candle right in the center of the poop, retreating quickly, without a word, back into the warmth of her apartment.

— JOHN SCOTT

My friend, Todd, was at my apartment one day and we were looking out my bedroom window onto the neighboring rooftop below. There were two women on the rooftop talking. All of a sudden, one of the women looks up and says, "Todd?" My friend looks down and says, "Laura?" They knew each other from a stage production in Cleveland, Ohio, years before.

— NS

One summer night, I was in my apartment and out of the corner of my eye I saw something pass by my window. A second later I heard what I thought was a watermelon smash into the pavement below with a hollow thud. Within minutes sirens came screaming up the street. I looked out and it turned out to be a jumper.

— CAROL FIORINO

On 7th Ave. a stranger shouted, "Your wallet's been stolen. Look!" A fly guy strolled ahead, putting my wallet in one pocket and my cash in the other. I ran up and yelled, "Give me back my wallet!" He complied, nervously. "Now give me all the money!" I said. With a few choice words he handed it over, and I unwittingly walked away with more money than I'd started out the day with.

— DONNA BRODIE

5 Pointz

A warehouse in Queens that invites artful vandalism.

Where: Jackson Ave., between Crane and Davis Sts., Long Island City, Queens
When: Viewing anytime; Painting: Saturday–Sunday, 12–7 p.m.
Getting there: E, V to 23 St./Ely Ave.; 7 or G to 45 Rd./Court House Square
Fee: Free
Website: 5ptz.com

5 Pointz—the free public outdoor gallery in Long Island City—has been showcasing major installations of graffiti art since 2001. Once known as the Phun Phactory, and now called the Institute of Higher Burnin', 5 Pointz is a massive playground for artists, covering a full city block. Roughly located at the geographical epicenter of the five boroughs, this cluster of abandoned warehouses and vandalized factories has been turned into a complex of artist studios and galleries and has become a magnet not only for graffiti artists but also hip hop fans, photographers, filmmakers, rappers and break dancers from around the world.

Legend has it that the golden age of graffiti began in the early 1970s when a Washington Heights kid started "tagging" his nickname, TAKI 183 (a combination of his name, Demetaki, and his street, 183rd), all over the city. A 1971 article in the New York *Times* made him an overnight legend, and hundreds of copycats were soon competing for fame on building walls, subways cars and tunnels. Not until the mid-1980s, when the city instituted a zero tolerance policy and toughened its anti-graffiti laws, was the art displaced to sanctioned venues.

A visit to 5 Pointz gets your heart racing with the vibe of a wilder, more subversive time in the city. You will see impassioned message murals, ephemeral pieces in explosive colors, exaggerated portraits, and aerosol depictions of good battling evil, all in surreal scale. The fact that the wall, staircase and roof art here are constantly painted over and ever changing makes each visit fresh.

If you want to bomb some 5 Pointz real estate yourself, you will have to contact Meres One (see website) to ask permission. As founder and curator, he decides who gets a permit to spray paint at his colorful chaos gallery. He also ensures that the originators of this subculture—famous old school artists like Phase 2 or Fab Five Freddy—are always provided a concrete canvas for their famous tags, Bronx "bubble" lettering or Brooklyn "wildstyle" expressions.

Is it art or vandalism? While that argument continues between critics and cops, 5 Pointz remains a graffiti Mecca for artists who can express themselves without having to watch their backs.

Passing Peculiarity

LENIN STATUE

WHERE: ON THE ROOF OF 250 E. HOUSTON ST., BETWEEN AVES. A AND B
NOTE: VISIBLE FROM STREET, NO ROOF ACCESS.

Oddly out-of-place in the capitol of capitalism is the 18-foot bronze Lenin statue standing on the roof of the luxury "Red Square" apartment building on Houston Street and Avenue A (best visible from the west). The Soviet Union originally commissioned the work from sculptor Yuri Gerasimov, but after the Soviet collapse, the statue sat in a backyard in Russia until leftist developers Michael Shaoul and Michael Rosen purchased it and shipped it to America in 1994. Placing the Soviet leader 13 stories above the street was a marketing gimmick intended to create controversy and raise the building's visibility. Now the Soviet leader hails New York's proletariat masses, right hand high in salute, a sort of "red" parody of Lady Liberty.

Foot Heaven

A stranger's touch in Chinatown.

Where: 16 Pell St., between Bowery & Doyers Sts.
When: Monday–Sunday, 11 a.m.–12:30 a.m.
Phone: 212-962-6588
Getting there: J, M, Z, N, Q, R, W or 6 to Canal St.
or 4, 5, 6, J, M, Z to Chambers-Brooklyn Bridge/City Hall
Fee: $40 for one hour of foot reflexology

Something about Chinatown makes every one of its businesses seem, well, a little suspect. Waiters in restaurants seem angry with you and no one wants to answer your questions. Street vendors hawk goods in whispered tones, "Gucci? Fendi?" while shopkeepers disappear behind false walls in the outdoor markets. If you watch closely, you might witness a package move surreptitiously between several runners and shills before ending up in the hands of a nervous tourist.

Maybe that's why Foot Heaven massage parlor felt compelled to post a sign above its door declaring "Legitimate Business No Hanky Panky!"

Foot and back rub spots are ubiquitous in Chinatown, so you'd think New Yorkers had nothing better to do than get their aching dogs scrubbed and rubbed all day. Fact is, many of these tootsie parlors offer an excellent service. And they're astonishingly cheap—Foot Heaven delivers an hour's worth of happy feet for only $40. The reflexology practitioners work through pressure points that correspond to particular glands and organs, relieving tension, improving circulation and "promoting your body's natural functions.

For the more adventurous, full body massages are offered in private spaces in the back. Moaning and groaning can be heard from behind drawn curtains, but don't worry. These masseurs believe in digging deep, and the whimpering speaks of pain, not pleasure. Remember, this is a legitimate business. No hanky-panky.

Fort Tilden

Abandoned nuclear missile silos inches from your beach blanket.

Where: Within Gateway National Park, Queens
When: Dawn to dusk, every day
Phone: 718-318-4300
Getting there: 2 to Flatbush Ave. or A to Rockaway Park, transfer to the Q35 Green Bus Lines (ask to be dropped off at Fort Tilden). By car, take Flatbush over the Marine Parkway Bridge ($2.75 each way) and follow the signs. Park for free at the barracks, or park at the fisherman's lot with a fishing permit ($50, available at building 1 35 at Floyd Bennett Field or at the visitor's center at Jacob Riis Park). Fee: Free
Website: newyorkharborparks.org

Most people know that New York City has beaches. Coney Island possesses its cacophony of amusements, Brighton Beach its Russian sternness, and Rockaway its—well, its surliness. But fewer know of the deserted white sand beaches and the abandoned battlements of Fort Tilden.

Ping pong your way far enough down Flatbush Avenue, and eventually, humanity falls away. Rumble over the Marine Parkway Bridge, and on the other side, off to your right, you'll find a peculiar oasis. Fort Tilden offers two oddities: summer beaches as empty as the Outer Banks in winter, alongside the vestiges of U-boat threats and Cold War paranoia. No signs direct you to the ruins; the visitor's center at the adjacent Jacob Riis Park doesn't even provide a map. A visit requires an intrepid spirit and a sturdy constitution fit for hiking or biking through the wartime detritus.

Construction of the Fort Tilden battlements began in 1917, but World War II marked the beginning of a four-decade-long buildup of an escalating assortment of weaponry—cannons, naval rifles and, later, Nike Ajax and Hercules surface-to-air missiles armed with nuclear warheads. In 1974, the fort was deactivated and turned over to the National Parks Service. Today, hidden in the vegetation, you'll find the concrete fortifications and missile silos, while the former barracks now house the Rockaway Artist's Alliance and Theater Company.

A sandy road cuts through the center of 317 acres of adjacent wild dunes and opens up at two separate batteries, Battery Harris East and West. Technically, you're not supposed to enter these fortifications, but wiggle your way through the gates (with flashlight in hand) and inside you'll find fresh graffiti covering the walls. Wooden steps lead up to an earth berm surrounding Battery Harris East. At the top, you get a 360-degree view of Jamaica Bay, New York Harbor and the Manhattan skyline. Along the road running directly behind the beach, you'll notice a high dune. Find the narrow path through thick shrubbery, and follow it to the entrance of another battery, again featuring a gallery of graffiti inside.

After you've finished exploring, feel free to sunbathe on the beach, but swim at your own risk—the currents are strong and there are no lifeguards. Note that just beyond Fort Tilden, an anachronistic breed of New Yorker relaxes at the Silver Gull Beach Club, rubbing their round tan tummies, playing cards, and snapping for cabana boys to fetch them their cocktails (this is the real life beach club used in the filming of the classic, The Flamingo Kid).

FLOYD BENNETT FIELD

NYC's first airport, is now home to some fringy but fun-loving hobbyists.

Where: 50 Aviator Rd., Brooklyn
When: Visitor Center hours, 9 a.m.–5 p.m. every day
Phone: 718-338-3799
Getting there: 2 (and 5 at rush hour) to Flatbush Ave.; Q35 bus to the park
Website: nyharborparks.org/visit/flbe.html

On your way back into the city, stop at Floyd Bennett Field—New York City's first municipal airport, which looks much the same as it did at its opening in 1931. Once a barren island, Floyd Bennett remains distant, desolate and undisturbed by the glare of city lights. The hangars, terminal and control towers still stand, but today most of the planes flying overhead are of the tiny, remote-controlled variety. The sprawling recreational area offers a ridiculous array of activities, yet it never feels overrun.

Enthusiasts of every sort come here to indulge their passions. Model airplane groups use a former runway, while RC car nuts race on a specially built track. One of the hangars now houses an NHL-sized ice rink, rock-climbing wall, gymnastics gymnasium, food court and bar. Cyclists race here. Fisherman catch striped bass out of Jamaica Bay, while kayakers put in via the former seaplane ramp at Hangar B. Hangar B also houses the Historic Aircraft Restoration Project (volunteers on the projects will often pause to describe to visitors the work being done). And the action doesn't stop after dark. Amateur astrologers come here for night sky viewing, and many young campers sleep under the stars for the first time at Floyd Bennett's Ecology Village.

Off the beaten track, but hardly abandoned, Floyd Bennett Field is a happening hobby hub. But if you're still bored, go fly a kite. Seriously. It's the perfect place for that, too.

Gotham Girls Roller Derby

Speedy queens of pain hurting each other in hot pants.

Where: Check website for schedule
When: Check website for schedule
Phone: 888-830-2253
Fee: Tickets prices vary; check website
Website: gothamgirlsrollerderby.com

If you go to a Gotham Girls Roller Derby bout expecting irony—like burlesque wrestling on roller skates—forget it. You're going to witness a sport. A highly competitive, brutal sport with rules. The program states the official rules, but you'll have to pay attention to the action to understand them. No-nonsense referees stand at the ready, along with EMTs, coaches and managers, too.

Best of all, there are the girls—true athletes. Amazonian women with thigh muscles that could bend rebar. Tiny powerhouses that can flash past opponents and juke incoming blocks. They wear mouthpieces, knee pads, elbow protectors and helmets—because they need them. They suffer injuries, sacrifice free time for practice time, and frequently walk into their day jobs with shiners and other casualties of the game. And none of them gets paid a cent. *That's* passion.

That said, the fishnet-and-hot-pants uniforms don't hurt attendance any. No matter the build, whether burly or stacked, each girl's outfit features a sexy touch; boobies bouncing in low-cut tops and muscled booties peaking out of ruffled bloomers.

Roller derby began during the Depression and finally waned in the 1970s. The current revival began in 2000 in Austin, Texas, and New York's Gotham Girls Roller Derby league joined the fray in 2003. The basic objective then as now is for one select skater (called a jammer) from a team of five to try to lap the skaters on the opposing team while circling a track. Previous incarnations involved pratfalls and much vamping, and today's skaters' campy style pays homage to the roller derby queens of the 1950s. Players take on alter-ego identities like Miss American Thighs, Anais Ninja, and Kandy Kakes.

Roller derby today—a grassroots, not-for-profit, ladies-doin'-it-for-themselves endeavor—has eliminated the earlier sexual spectacles that included spanking the players in the penalty box. The leagues found that audiences initially came in hopes of seeing a boob fly out during a spill, but they stayed for the athleticism. The coaches scream from the benches, the refs closely follow the action, and EMTs are on hand for moments when women get hit and fall hard. During a recent bout, several players took blocks squarely and flew off of the track, arms and legs flailing, heavy skates jamming the dainty feet of those in the trackside VIP seats. Several players were benched with obvious injuries, wearing casts, braces and slings. Torn ACLs, shattered legs, and broken collarbones are not uncommon.

Gotham Girls features four teams, the Queens of Pain, Brooklyn Bombshells, Bronx Gridlock, and Manhattan Mayhem, plus the traveling Wall Street Traitors and the Gotham Girls All Stars. But the roller derby community appears more a tribe than a bunch of warring factions. All of the players participate in the running of the league. At the end of the games, opposing teams will mingle and embrace one another. No cliques pull away from the pack. They find no use for cattiness, timidity, or validation. They have fun, they are aggressive, they hurt each other, and then they leave it on the track. Tryouts are held every winter. Women readers, take note.

Passing Peculiarity

MOSAIC HOUSE

WHERE: 108 WYCOFF ST.,
BETWEEN HOYT AND
SMITH STS., BROOKLYN

As artist Susan Gardner states on her website, "One day in 2001, I went outside and started gluing things to the front of my house. I have not stopped yet." She incorporates tiles, brooches, buttons, plastic fruit, CDs, shells, crockery, beads and more. After nearly a decade, her mosaic has crept up the front of her building, encrusted the fence, and covered the walkway and front doorstep. Flowers bloom, couples dance, a woman perches over the doorframe. Each spring, when the weather breaks, Susan comes out to add more cheer to Boerum Hill. If you're lucky, she'll be out on her ladder, always open to a chat with strangers.

Green-Wood Cemetery

600,000 former New Yorkers dirt-napping beneath your feet.

Where: 500 25th St., at 5th Ave., Brooklyn
When: Open daily, 8 a.m.–5 p.m.
Phone: 718-768-7300
Getting there: R to 25th St. in Brooklyn. Walk east one block.
Fee: Free
Website: green-wood.com

If it weren't for the moldering corpses buried six feet under, Green-Wood Cemetery would seem positively cheerful—just a bucolic sculpture park perched atop the highest point in Brooklyn. A nesting colony of bright green monk parakeets greets you with screeches from the neo-Gothic sandstone gate, while winding roads meander over rolling terrain, creating the feel of a pastoral jaunt. Lavishly designed crypts and storied epitaphs make for a lovely, yet strange day in this necropolis of 600,000 and counting.

David Bates Douglas intended these effects when he laid out the landscape design in the 1830s. A precursor to the public park, Green-Wood served not only as a place to mourn the dead but also to mourn the passing of agrarian life. Nostalgic urbanites came here to picnic on the well fertilized ground and tour the ornate monuments—in fact, throughout the 19th Century Green-Wood was the second most popular tourist destination in New York State, just behind Niagara Falls.

Some of the most famous New Yorkers of the late 1800s made their final home here, and their stories often intertwined. Consider the particularly massive tomb belonging to 17-year-old Charlotte Canda—a socialite who tragically died the night of her debutante ball in 1845 by falling from a runaway carriage, cracking her head open on the pavement. Her fiancé lies nearby, having committed suicide at the Canda residence of her parents just a year after her death.

There's abolitionist Henry Ward Beecher, who made headlines for bedding his best friend's wife, Elizabeth Tilton. His trial for adultery became the first "trial of the century." Upon her death, and seeking to provide some anonymity to the hounded Elizabeth Tilton, her family marked her grave near the Battle Hill monument with the vague inscription "grandmother." Beecher himself rests at a distance, near the Hillside Mausoleum. Another twist: at the other end of the graveyard, near the Green-Wood chapel, lies fervent anti-abolitionist and Alabama Senator Dixon Hall Louis.

Stories of murder and tragedy abound concerning this underground population. William "Bill the Butcher" Poole, the infamous Bowery Boys gang member of the 1850s, rotted in an unmarked grave until the 2002 Martin Scorcese film *Gangs of New York* prompted a proper headstone. Crazy Joey Gallo ended up here after gunmen rubbed him out at Umberto's Clam House in 1972. At the monument to the Brooklyn Theater Fire of 1876, the bodies of 103 unidentified or destitute victims were buried, arranged in a crescent shape with their heads toward the monument. Sculptures of lambs and sleeping babies mark the graves of children, memorializing a common Victorian-era tragedy.

Familiar names behind global icons reside here, too, like pencil pusher Eberhard Faber (in a #2 coffin?); piano magnate Henry Steinway; the soap king William Colgate; and inventor of the sewing machine Elias Howe, buried with his dog, Fannie. Of course, you're forced to click your heels three times at the tombstone of actor Frank Morgan, moviedom's Wizard of Oz.

Though the economic downturn of the '70s wreaked havoc on Green-Wood, forcing it to close its gates for a time, the cemetery once again serves its original purpose. Visitors still come to tour the grounds and gawk at death. There's an appropriately creepy moonlight tour every so often. And around Halloween, Green-Wood historian Jeff Richman leads well-attended murder and mayhem tours.

WOODLAWN CEMETERY
One happening place to rot.

Where: Webster Ave. & E. 233rd St., Bronx
When: Open daily, 8:30 a.m.–4:30 p.m.
Phone: 718-920-0500; Toll Free, 877-496-6352
Getting there: 4 to Woodlawn; 2, 5 to 233rd St.
Website: thewoodlawncemetery.org

If your morbid obsession hasn't been sated at Green-Wood, head over to The Bronx for New York's other premier resting place. Woodlawn Cemetery, located in what was once the rural northernmost edge of the five boroughs, became the happening place to decay for celebrities and show-biz types. Duke Ellington lies just across the road from Miles Davis. Irving Berlin, Damon Runyon, and George M. Cohan found their final home here, as did Ziegfried girl and silver-screen star Martha Mansfield, who met a tragic end when her hoop skirt caught fire by a lit cigarette while filming The Warrens of Virginia.

Designed in 1868, Woodlawn follows a Landscape Lawn Plan, which encouraged grand monuments and mausoleums. The landscaping created a competition among many wealthy families for the most ostentatious crypts, many of which boast Grecian columns and bold sculptures, e.g the twin sphinxes flanking the Woolworth mausoleum. This non-sectarian cemetery has interred more than 300,000 people. With so many dead people to choose from, you're sure to find someone you like.

Guss' Pickles and Pickle Guys

Follow the sound of a century old "snap"
on the Lower East Side.

Guss's Pickles
Where: 39th St., between 14th and 15th Aves. in Borough Park, Brooklyn

Pickle Guys
Where: 49 Essex St. below Grand St.; also, 1364 Coney Island Ave.,
on the corner of Avenue J, Brooklyn
When: Sunday–Thursday, 9 a.m.–6 p.m.; Fri, 9 a.m.–4 p.m.
Phone: 212-656-9739 (Brooklyn, 718-677-0639)
Getting there: F, J, M, Z to Delancey St.; F to East Broadway;
B, D to Grand St.
Website: pickleguys.com

Eating an authentic Kosher pickle plucked from a barrel on the Lower East Side is like mainlining the briny blood of the city itself. If you track down nothing else in this book, get yourself a good pickle. The best of the best are Guss' Pickles and the Pickle Guys—indisputably the two kings of cured cucumbers.

Recently, Guss' Pickles got itself into a legal pickle and was forced to move. Turns out another Guss' Pickles opened in Cedarhurst, NY, and engaged the Lower East Side Guss' in a lawsuit over trademark ownership. No matter: the Guss' Pickles that New York has known and loved since 1920 lived in barrels on the sidewalk of the LES for 90 years. Now they have conveniently rolled their barrels to 39th Street, between 14th and 15th Avenues in Borough Park, Brooklyn, a largely Orthodox Jewish neighborhood.

Fortunately, pickle man Alan Kaufman saw the demise of New York's sidewalk, barrel-cured sour pickles coming a few years ago. A former pickle poker for Guss', he opened Pickle Guys, which arguably produces a barrel-cured sour pickle superior to that of his former boss. His Kirby cucumbers get placed in barrels of saltwater seasoned with garlic and spices. A "new" pickle is one that has sat in its spicy bath for a day, while half sours, three-quarters sours, and full sours can cure for up to six months. Pickle Guys also offers hot pickles, pickled tomatoes, a variety of olives as well as sweet kraut and sauerkraut, all dietary staples of the immigrants who once lived in neighborhood tenements.

Most days, a line spills out the door of Pickle Guys onto the street, where just a few decades ago as many as six different pickle sellers sold their preserved cukes. You can now find Kaufman, a man with a perpetual smile, tending his store six days a week, informing passersby that "on a hot day, a new pickle refreshes," and making sure that the century-old aroma of garlic and brine hangs in a heady cloud over the LES. Just like it always did. Just like it should be.

YONAH SCHIMMEL'S KNISH BAKERY

Eat, eat...come on, one more bite.

Where: 137 East Houston St., between 1st and 2nd Aves.
When: Sunday–Thursday, 9 a.m.–7 p.m.;
Friday–Saturday, 9 a.m.–9 p.m.
Phone: 212-477-2858
Website: knishery.com

While Jewish people make up 1.5 percent of the population in America, they account for 12 percent of all New Yorkers. From 1881 to 1914, nearly two million Eastern European Jews poured into America, many into New York, and most of those into the Lower East Side tenements. The neighborhood quickly became one of the most densely populated areas in the world. It was through these teeming streets that Yonah Schimmel began pedaling his knishes from a pushcart in 1890.

A knish traditionally consists of boiled buckwheat groats (kasha) or mashed potatoes wrapped in dough, baked and served hot. Hardly a deli in New York goes without this belly-busting snack behind the counter, but only a few true knisheries remain. Yonah Schimmel's Knish Bakery ranks as one of the best, if not the city's top knisherie. In its current location since 1910, Schimmel's still retains its original misspelled signage (Yonah Shimmel), its tiled ceiling, glass display cases, and fist-sized pies, save a few flavors that have been added to cater to the modern palate.

Order the kasha or the potato if it's your first visit. This gourmand destination isn't going anywhere. You can get the sweet potato next time.

Hidden Harbor Tour

*An awe-inspiring tribute to rusting metal, nautical
paint and longshoremen.*

Where: Pier 16 at South Street Seaport
When: Four times every summer
Getting there: 2, 3, 4, 5, J, Z, M to Fulton St., walk east
Fee: $29
Website: workingharbor.com

One offbeat tour leads its participants deep into the netherworld of steel, oil drums and metal heaps that form the industrial backdrop of the New York waterfront. Four times a year the people of the Working Harbor Committee pull back the curtain on the third largest port in the country on their Hidden Harbor Tour. You'll get an intimate look at the grimacing toilers of the bay, a subculture of authentic New Yorkers performing a clockwork operation as artful as any performance at Lincoln Center.

Working Harbor consists of folks with varied interests in the harbor, from wanting to protect their livelihoods to preserving the Harbor's heritage. Capt. John Doswell, an energetic advocate of all things nautical in the city, hosts the tour along with a guest—usually a professional from the shipping industry or a maritime historian. The tour boat embarks at sunset from Pier 16 at the South Street Seaport. It floats south, past the Brooklyn piers and Governor's Island before circling through Erie Basin (home of Ikea and Red Hook's beloved Fairway supermarket).

From there, you cross the Upper New York Harbor, passing moored tankers that wait for barges or docking tugboats. The tour moves further south, through Kill Van Kull, past Snug Harbor in Staten Island (see page 90)

on your left and Bayonne, NJ to your right (yes, Bayonne is on the tour...
now you're getting the idea). When it passes under the fixed Bayonne
Bridge, visitors learn that the span is too vertically challenged to accommodate today's colossal vessels, causing super-shipping companies to lose
significant dollars because they can't deliver that extra stack of containers.

Many consider the waterfront areas of Brooklyn, New Jersey and Staten
Island to be some of the most unsightly stretches in the country. But to
see all that ugliness close up can make a person fall in love with the shipping
industry, not to mention the seedier sides of New Jersey. Tugs gently
nudge container ships into port, while tall cranes pluck off the metal boxes
and stack them neatly in the sprawling yards that stretch 25 football fields
wide and deep.

The tour circles through Newark Bay and returns through Kill Van Kull,
where you get an excellent view of the Military Ocean Terminal and ships
being painted in the graving dock. The paint creates a ghostly mist around
the hulking gray ships. There you can also see the 9/11 Teardrop Memorial,
a gift from the Russians. Oddly, few people but dockworkers and ships'
crews ever cast eyes on it.

Hua Mei Bird Garden

*A 600-year-old morning ritual involving Chinamen
and birdsong on the LES.*

**Where: Just south of Delancey St. at Forsythe St. in the
Sarah Delano Roosevelt Park
When: Every morning from 7 a.m. to Noon, early spring to late fall
Getting there: B, D to Grand; F, V to Second Ave.
Fee: Free**

In an anonymous city like New York, people often seek like-minded tribes
and create sacred spaces in which to meet. The tribe of several dozen men
in Chinatown huddles around songbirds and communes in a half-moon of
tranquility at the foot of Sara Delano Roosevelt Park.

On any morning of the week, from early spring to late fall, they are there.
The elderly men, many retired from careers in nearby restaurants, sit along
a wall, smoking and chatting, rising every so often to check on their prized
possessions. The Hua Mei birds, a fighting thrush, hop about in ornate
bamboo cages. When in the presence of a female, the males warble a vast
repertoire of melodies. The men simply sip their coffee and appreciate
the songs that rise above the hum of the Lower East Side.

This unique gathering began in the '80s, when a group of men would carry their caged Hua Mei songbirds on daily walks through the park. Back then, a specialty pet store at the corner of Delancey provided the men with live crickets for the voracious cagelings. The tribe officially received its home in 1995, when several men decided to reclaim a portion of the park from tottering junkies and prostitutes. With the blessing of the city, they planted Asiatic shrubs and berry bushes in their sacred corner and outfitted it with a clothesline from which to hang their cages.

Less eccentric than devoted to a tradition that dates back to the Ming Dynasty in China, the men spend up to $1000 on the Hua Mei, just to enjoy their robust melodies. For passersby, the idea of it seems as foreign as the fruit in the street stalls of Chinatown. But for these men, the birds provide comfort and familiarity amid a land of mysterious tongues and habits. In a city that purges history daily, you can only hope that this tradition has its heirs.

Jacques Marchais Museum of Tibetan Art

What's on your lamasery altar?

Where: 338 Lighthouse Ave., Staten Island
When: Thursday–Sunday, 1–5 p.m.; Sunday's last admission 4:30 p.m.
(winter and summer schedule vary slightly)
Phone: 718-987-3500
Getting there: From Manhattan, take Staten Island Ferry to Staten Island,
then S74 bus (meets every ferry) to Lighthouse Ave. Walk up the hill
(5–10 minutes) to the Museum. Bus takes approximately 30 mins.
Fee: $5
Website: tibetanmuseum.org

Where are you going to see the largest number of gilded Buddhas, ornate prayer wheels, elaborate incense burners, and authentic Tibetan art outside of the remote Asian country itself? If you guessed Staten Island (and you didn't), you should be on Jeopardy.

We have Jacqueline Klauber to thank for this cliff-clinging tribute to a Tibetan mountain temple (she employed the name Jacques Marchais professionally because it facilitated purchase of her art in the 1930s and 1940s). The New York art dealer was obsessed with Tibetan and Himalayan art and wanted to have it close to her home in Staten Island. Hence, this monastery museum, with an awesomely jam-packed lamasery altar, houses one of the largest collections of Tibetan art in the free world.

The museum, located in a former private home in a residential area, sits at the highest point on the eastern seaboard with terrific views of the distant New York harbor. In the pleasant patio garden there are stone baboons, elephants and rabbits, too, with cheerful live goldfish in the requisite lotus pond.

Jim Power's Mosaic Trail

Miles of tiles from the tenacious Mosaic Man.

Where: On 8th St. and St. Marks, between Broadway and Ave. A for the best viewing; also, on Ave. A from St. Marks St. to E. 4th St. and on E. 4th St from Avenue A to Broadway; also, Crif Dogs bathroom
When: Whenever you want

At times New York City seems anarchic —a roiling pot of artistic expression and punk rock ethos—and the suspension of rules is good for the soul. But when the Byzantine Empire that is our city government chooses to, it can steamroll all the fun. Or sometimes, it just paints over it, as in the case of Jim Power's Mosaic Trail.

Back in 1985, Power, a Vietnam vet and resident of the East Village, decided to mark the boundaries of his neighborhood, which then was a hotbed of junkies, thieves, and gangsters. Armed with a hammer, Power stole into the wild night to cement little riots of color on dull gray lampposts. Over the next 25 years, he created 80 mosaics along the route and became an East Village icon. The mosaics pay homage to the police and fire departments, honor civil rights and patriotic pride, and memorialize events such as 9/11 and the Blackout of '03. Tourists delight as they happen upon one after another, on planters, embedded in sidewalks, and even in the bathroom of Crif Dogs wiener restaurant.

Power, a.k.a. the Mosaic Man, claims to have poured $100,000 into his project. In recent years, the maintenance of his work has proven difficult, now that a bad hip and a cash shortage hobble his efforts. Intermittently homeless, he has scraped by on his sale of the eastvillage.com domain name, as well as through handouts and the occasional commissioned work. While neighborhood devotees have made attempts to preserve his creations, the city refuses to recognize his contribution as a landmark. As the mosaics decay, the city paints over them, the lumpy remnants hinting that something beautiful once transformed each corner. Only twenty mosaics remain intact.

Power recently proclaimed his project dead. On his rambling blog, he wrote, "What a waste of my time, for what?" That's sad, because this man and his art embody the beating heart of New York. At some point, the city has to realize that luxury condos can't define us. Humanity doesn't paint on cave walls for nothing.

Las Tunas Botanica

Black magic remedy shop for the devil in you.

Where: 112 Nagle Ave., Inwood
When: Daily, 10 a.m.-8 a.m.
Getting there: 1 to Dyckman St.

Protect yourself from the devil, bring back a lost lover, exact vengeance on an enemy. Sound like voodoo? You'll find out at Las Tunas Botanica, in the heart of uptown Inwood.

Not many neighborhoods in Manhattan still retain the edge and eccentricity that have drawn people to the city for decades. But in Inwood you can still hear gunshots being fired in celebration after an intense baseball game or walk into a building's basement to see a neighbor skinning a deer.

Las Tunas Botanica is located in a colorful neighborhood where Caribbean immigrants often sit outdoors and play dominoes to the sound of salsa and merengue. A "botanica" is a folk-medicine store stocked with religious articles as well as many items that may seem mysterious and strange to the uninitiated. There are several botanicas in the area, but Las Tunas has the most exhaustive display of amulets, potions and mystical charms.

Many of these unusual items are used during the rituals of "Santeria," an Afro-Caribbean religion based on traditional beliefs originating in Nigeria. The rituals can involve offerings to saints, dancing, invocations, and animal sacrifices—with some participants falling into deep trance states. And everyone gets their Santeria supplies at Las Tunas.

As you step through the shop's door you are humbled by two towering plastic statues of saints, their feet festooned with money. The air smells of incense, garlic and other aromatic plants. Every inch of the wall space is covered with shelves lined with thousands of items placed in irregular rows: bath oils, ointments, and glass-encased candles tossed together with plaster figurines of saints and angels, goats, horses and other mystical animals. Hanging from the ceiling is an eclectic collection of rosaries, bells, calabashes and bracelets. Sometimes incantations can be heard coming from a back room, whispered in an unrecognizable dialect.

Behind the counter at Las Tunas, not far from a human skull (it may be plastic, but you never know), powders are sold that promise to grant your wishes post haste. You could probably obtain the necessary ingredients for black magic here, too—but you'd have to ask nicely.

Images of bubbling cauldrons come to mind as you browse through the intriguing collection of colorful liquids with curious labels: *Amarra hombre* (tie your man), *Espanta muerto* (scare death away), *Rechaza baño* (repel harm), and *Contra el diablo* (counter the devil). Other bottles are more mysterious: *Abre camino* (open the path) or *Lagrimas de hombres* (men's tears).

Regulars often visit Las Tunas several times a month (you can never get enough protection from the devil in New York City), and it's always crowded with clients purchasing noxious-smelling potions for problems of love, money or revenge. If you want to get in touch with your inner witch doctor, Las Tunas will have exactly the potent powders you need to, say, grow rat's ears on your ex.

Passing Peculiarity

RALPH KRAMDEN FROM THE HONEYMOONERS

WHERE: WEST SIDE OF 8TH AVE., BETWEEN 40TH AND 41STS.

He threatened to send Alice to the moon for most of our childhoods (and even now on cable's TV Land), but Jackie Gleason as Brooklyn bus driver Ralph Kramden looks fairly jovial here with lunchbox in hand and potbelly held high. The 8-ft. tall bronze statue stands in front of (what else?) The Port Authority Bus Terminal, where it's easily missed in the shadows of an entrance overhang. Dedicated in 2000, the Ralph statue was funded by TV Land in cooperation with the Port Authority and Gleason's estate. Of course, if they ever wanted to move this tribute to 50's television, there's one other place it would feel at home...in front of the Raccoon Lodge in Tribeca.

Life Underground

A weird world of bronze busybodies stops you on the subway.

Where: 14th St. A, C, E Subway Stop
When: 24 hours, daily
Fee: Free
Website: mta.info/mta/aft/permanentart

Art abounds in the New York City subway system, thanks to a law that requires one percent of all public construction budgets to be used for public art. One of the most curious results is Tom Otterness's 2002 installation Life Underground, found peeking from corners throughout the 14th St. A, C, E subway stop. The cartoonish bronze sculptures, over 100 in all, resemble both Rich Uncle Pennybags (a.k.a. the Monopoly Guy) and the doozers of Fraggle Rock (come on, you remember them).

The pieces create a perfect allegory for life above ground in this feral hub of wealth and power. Below one stairwell, you see a man-eating lobster. Under another, a figure with a moneybag head scrambles in vain to escape the jaws of an alligator. Look up, and you'll see half a dozen characters installing an I-beam. At your feet, fare-jumpers crawl beneath the turnstile as a police figure looks on. In a quiet corner, a lady cop accosts a sleeping figure. An elephant and a donkey go head-to-head as commuters descend the stairs below. The installation evokes the influence of money, the lack of it, the preponderance of it, the use and abuse of it.

Unfortunately, Tom Otterness has a history that will forever tarnish his reputation as a serious artist. In 1977, he adopted a dog and shot it to death, an act he recorded on video and replayed on a loop and called it art. In the modern style, he issued a short apology in 2008, and then continued getting commissioned for more public works.

What was the theme of this subway installation? Ah, yes, the corrupting pursuit of money and fame.

The Living Museum

Art imitates life, in all its excruciating glory.

**Where: Creedmoor Psychiatric Center, 79-25 Winchester Blvd.,
Queens Village
When: By appointment only
Phone: 718-264-4000
Getting there: E to Union Tpke–Kew Gardens Station,
Q46 bus to Union Tpke–Winchester Blvd.
Fee: Free
Website: omh.state.ny.us/omhweb/facilities/crpc/facility.htm**

The most honest, individual, passionate and curious art in New York sits not in the Whitney, at a Chelsea gallery, or in the studios of the city's numerous art schools. Instead, you'll have to travel by train, bus and foot to Building 75 on the sprawling complex of the Creedmoor Psychiatric Center. Within the confines of these four walls, the artists of The Living Museum electrify the air with exuberant and prolific creativity.

The approach to Creedmoor intimidates with a tall chain-link fence, looming architecture, and a landscape dotted with abandoned, ivy-covered buildings. As you enter the grounds, the presence of perhaps one or two people punctuates otherwise empty acreage. Creedmoor once housed 7,000 patients. Today, only a few hundred in-patients remain, due in part to deinstitutionalization efforts (a result of complex factors), and also thanks to the miracles of pharmaceutical drug therapy.

Building 75 also once sat empty and derelict, inhabited by squirrels, paint peeling off the walls and ceilings, floors swirling with leaves and debris. In 1983, Polish artist Boleck Greczinski and Dr. Janos Marton saw an opportunity and set about transforming the building into a comforting space for patients to produce art. While the Living Museum wasn't the first art therapy program, Creedmoor became the first psychiatric center in the U.S. to systematically collect art produced by patients.

Greczinski passed away in 1995, but Dr. Marton remains the Museum's dedicated steward. At first glance, Building 75 appears abandoned still, but then, under a shady walkway, a group of men gathers and talks. Behind them, a patch of sunshine illuminates a garden with a tree that has been painted in bright hues, its branches hung with blackened wood ornaments. A nearby doorway is lined with relief sculptures.

Inside, Dr. Marton chats amiably with the artists, interacting with them as a professor might with his students rather than as a therapist with his patients. Yet, the artists are in- or out-patients, many of whom were assigned to

Creedmoor by the courts. They suffer from schizophrenia, drug-induced psychosis, debilitating depression and delusional states, among other diagnoses. But their illnesses, while at times providing context, do not undermine each artist's ability to create moving works that can be judged on their own merit.

Expressionist paintings, installation art, abstract sculptures and collages occupy every room, hang from the rafters and emerge from every corner of The Living Museum. In fact, Dr. Marton has called the entire museum a work of conceptual art. It invites the question of what is art, and to what extent does all art come from a portion of the mind that leads to mental illness. The Living Museum sits in the center of society's Venn Diagram, with so-called normal people in one circle, so-called crazy people in the other, and art the center where the two worlds overlap. As art can serve as a mirror for life, a trip to this space can be unsettling, drawing us nearer to unmitigated emotion, to existential curiosity, to brutal honesty.

But isn't that how you feel after you view great art?

Liz Christy Bowery-Houston Garden

The city's first community garden is a shrine to green activism.

Where: Northeast corner of Houston and Bowery Sts.
When: Saturday, Noon–4 p.m. (year-round); Sunday, Noon–4 p.m.
(May to October); Tuesday, 6 p.m.–Dusk (May to October)
Phone: 212-594-2155
Getting there: D, F to Broadway/Lafayette St.
Website: greenguerillas.org

You can walk by this stubborn little community garden and not even realize it's there, such are the distractions of the tightly pressed world around it. But step through its gate and you quickly understand why the protectors of this sliver of verdancy fight to keep it green.

More than 700 community gardens exist in the city, but there would be a lot fewer if it hadn't been for the work and vision of Liz Christy. In 1973, the local resident created the Green Guerillas, a volunteer group that went around neighborhoods in the Village and SoHo removing trash from vacant, decaying lots and "seed bombing" naked tree pits.

When Christy saw the possibilities for the large rubble-strewn parcel on Houston Street, she got the city to agree to rent the space, soon to be called the Bowery Houston Farm and Garden, for $1 a month. Volunteer groups from all over the city soon saw what the stubborn Christy and her stalwart army of guerilla volunteers were doing downtown and copied her. The rest is history.

Despite some nasty encroachments on the cloistered oasis in recent years, like massive reconstruction of Houston Street to its south and the development of a towering apartment along its north wall, this community garden unflinchingly survives. A volunteer labor force lovingly tends to sixty beds filled with vegetables, fruit trees, and fragrant herbs. The garden also has a goldfish and turtle pond, a beehive and a grape arbor. A small stand of birch trees and a low berm overflowing with robust wild flowers does a remarkable job of drowning out the incessant thrum of Houston Street traffic.

If you want a quick encounter with nature in one of the most unlikely places on the planet, step into the Liz Christy garden. By all accounts, this garden shouldn't be here. But because of some inspired green activism, it is here. To stay.

Passing Peculiarity

RATS ON THE GRAYBAR

WHERE: 420 LEXINGTON AVE., NEXT TO GRAND CENTRAL

Rats have infiltrated every building in New York. So it should come as no surprise to find three of them racing up each of the canopy supports for the Graybar Building, which is adjacent to Grand Central Terminal. (People often think this entrance is for Grand Central.) Anti-rat devices thwart each metallic rodent, while a rosette of eight rat heads awaits at the end of each of the bronze hawser lines. Built in 1927, the Graybar served as a symbol of New York's central role in the (apparently rat-infested) maritime shipping industry. Today, it is quite possibly the only building in the world to incorporate a rat motif into its architecture.

Only in New York Stories 2

When I was a teenager I worked in a health food store on the Upper East Side and we were once robbed at gunpoint. I never thought the guy would be caught or that I'd hear any more about him. But a year later we heard he held up another health food store, and the owner shot him dead. I guess he thought health nuts were peaceniks.

— Debra Stasi

*I was friendly with the renowned artist Raphael Soyer in the 1970's and 1980's. He was in his 80th decade when I knew him and he was quite short, maybe five feet tall or so. He lived in the same apartment building as Paul Simon, the famous songwriter musician. Upon finding himself eye-to-eye in the elevator one day with the younger celebrity, Raphael looked at Paul Simon and remarked, "I know who you are," to which Simon responded, "I know who **you** are." Nothing more was said.*

— NANCY RICA SCHIFF

I was with a friend in the late 60's on Avenue C and a crazed looking guy with a knife approached us and demanded our money. My friend said, to my horror, "You ain't getting my money so you better know how to use that thing." The mugger looked at my black friend (an ex-con and junkie), then at me (vertiginous collegiate Jew), before high tailing it back into the shadows.

— DAN BERNSTEIN

A man ran out of a bank on Broadway and 9th Street holding a bag. As he passed close by, the bag's dye pack exploded and covered him with red paint. The paint hit me and I thought I'd been shot. Knees weak, I sank to the sidewalk. He kept running and was caught about three blocks away.

— ADAM IBEL

I was standing on a street corner in Brooklyn Heights at a public phone holding an almost empty cup of water in my hand. I was dressed in shorts and a dirty t-shirt. A passerby dropped some change in my cup and kept on walking. I was too surprised and busy talking on the phone to inform him that I was NOT, in fact, looking for a handout!

— STEVE ZABIN

Manhattan Night Court

Our city justice system at its worst finest hour.

Where: 100 Centre St.
When: Seven days a week, 5 p.m.–1 a.m.
Getting there: 6, J, M, Z to Canal St.
Note: Pho Viet Huong restaurant is located at 73 Mulberry St.

Misery may love company, but it probably doesn't appreciate an audience. Too bad for the defendants marched through Manhattan's night court— their worst hour is on display for friends, family, all the public and even visiting tourists to see.

Once upon a time, people could be held for four or five days in New York City awaiting arraignment. However in 1991, the criminal court system fell in line with the Constitution, and people would forever after be charged in a court of law within 24 hours of their arrest. This led to a 24/7 criminal court. In 2003, arrests dropped off and the late-late shift (1 a.m. to 9 a.m.) ended, but the evening entertainment remains in place seven days a week from 5 p.m. to 1 a.m., when court clerks shuffle in the pettiest of criminals, still reeling from the dramatic circumstances that landed them in jail.

The U.S. court system, in contrast to many countries, holds its proceedings in full view of the public. The result is a reality show like no other. Couples come on dates. Europeans, obsessed with gun-slinging America, cement their preconceptions by watching the accused suffer Jerry Springer-like humiliation.

One after another, the defendants file in from the holding cell behind the judge's bench. They slouch on a row of seats until their attorney calls them into a sort of glass confessional. Then they file back to their seats until the bailiff, a jovial guy as entertained by the proceedings as any onlooker, calls their case. One weary judge on a September evening, her long, wiry gray hair framing sorrowful eyes, looked down on each of the accused with empathy.

A slumped heroin addict was reminded of his 23 other misdemeanors and his last girlfriend who'd OD'ed. Next, a boy, just 15, was charged with assault and robbery. The judge called up the mother, who cried as she listened to the weight of the charges. Serious drug charges for three young men resulted in $10,000 bonds. Their three girlfriends, for some reason all dressed in red, waited expectantly in the audience. Two cried while the bail was set, while one stormed out in a rage.

Poor acoustics swallow half of the dialogue, but often the trial participants pantomime their roles. The attorney shakes his head and waves some papers, raising his hands in a shrug. The prosecutor riffles through the rap sheet, looking for reasons to raise the bail. The defendants shake, slouch or mumble—most numb with weariness, fear or confusion. The narratives are so compelling you find yourself eager to see how things end for the attractive Asian shoplifter in her A-line dress, the African-American boy already looking resigned to a miserable fate, or the man who showed up in court in his pajamas.

It's hard to feel good about your voyeuristic status or the human compulsion to watch train wreck after train wreck pass through the courtroom. But it is legal to attend and it's free. Court breaks for dinner at 9 p.m. And there's a great Vietnamese place right around the corner.

M iss Vera's Finishing School For Boys Who Want To Be Girls

America's first transvestite training ground.

Where: Chelsea studio (Call for directions)
When: By appointment
Phone: 212-242-6449
Fee: Varies
Website: missvera.com

Veronica Vera is the woman behind the men in bras and panties.

Since the early 1990's, her famous cross-dressing academy—the first in the world and the only one with a full faculty—has shown thousands of closeted transgender men how to stand up for themselves … without falling over in their stilettos.

An estimated three to five percent of the male population likes to wear women's clothing from time to time and, according to Miss Vera, it is this "venus envy" that pulls hundreds of men from around the world to her Chelsea studio every year. About 20 percent of her clients are New Yorkers, another 25 percent are European, and the rest come from places where a man wearing an A-line skirt in public might get his wig knocked off, or worse.

"New York's tolerant, live-and-let-live attitude makes it the ideal place for the academy," says Miss Vera. "It's also a great walking city, and men who dress up want to walk around and be seen. In this city, they're not only seen, they're admired." Miss Vera tells the story of one transvestite client who wanted to be a bride for a day, so the academy created a bachelorette party for her (uhh, him) in a downtown restaurant. At one point a straight woman from a neighboring table came over to compliment the bride-to-not-be on her faux engagement ring. Says Miss Vera, "My client was thrilled."

Most of the tranny explorers who visit the academy choose a popular two-hour class that includes the cross-dressing transformation (plenty of frocks, coifs, perfumes and pumps to choose from), full makeup from a professional makeup artist, a photo session, and a walk through nearby streets and into shops for everyday interactions. While many of her clients have been dressing in women's clothing since childhood, this is typically their first time being transformed by pros who make them feel proud to look fabulous in public.

Miss Vera also emphasizes that her clients are not perverts (most are businessman, with a high concentration of lawyers) and the experience is not about sex, but rather gender. They are there because they want to live the academy's motto—"Cherchez la femme"—to find their feminine self and discover their unique look in drag.

If you're eager to cherchez your own femme, you should know that Miss Vera's Finishing School is not inexpensive. The complete cross-dressing class mentioned above costs around $450. For that, men get the wig and the wardrobe, lots of pampering and professional guidance, and they get to let the inner girl out, in style. Which can be very liberating when you've had your favorite little black dress stashed in the back of your closet for a decade with no chance to show it off.

Mole People and The Freedom Tunnel

A sketchy subterranean world where only the bravest dare go.

Where: Down below (Freedom Tunnel entrance near 125th St. and Riverside Park)

It's no myth—mole people do exist, although the term needs explaining. During the '70s, '80s, and '90s, hordes of homeless people took to New York City's subway tunnels to escape the sweltering heat and bitter cold of the outdoors, as well as the thieves and junkies of the city's shelters. These alienated souls found themselves living not on the wrong side of the tracks, but under, over or alongside them. Though most were driven out during Mayor Giuliani's era, today an unknown number continue to homestead the enclaves along unused or under-used tracks. They are victims of shitty breaks, a rash of poor decisions, addiction or mental illness, and arguably, a social system that has failed them.

Jennifer Toth's 1995 book, *The Mole People: Life in the Tunnels Beneath New York City*, purportedly chronicled her forays into this underworld, but critics have pointed out many glaring inaccuracies, calling into question the book's veracity. Regardless, *The Mole People*, using unverifiable quotes from folks who appear to be off their meds, perpetrated the myth of underground societies inhabited by a species of web-footed humanoids. A far more believable view is presented in the award-winning 2000 documentary, *Dark Days*. A true gonzo journalist, first-time director Mark

Singer lived among his subjects for months in a shantytown dubbed the Freedom Tunnel, which runs adjacent to Riverside Park from 125th Street to Penn Station. The tunnel remains but the shantytown has been bulldozed.

Intrepid urban explorers can access the Freedom Tunnel through a semi-hidden entrance in Riverside Park at 125th Street. You do so at your own risk (meaning, don't come suing the city, or these authors, if you get clobbered, rolled or sexuality assaulted). Once submerged, watch out for discarded needles, not to mention the Amtrak trains that hurtle along the tracks. Oh, and keep your eyes peeled for menacing types.

The payoff: hills of archaeological remnants from where the shantytown once stood and some of the best graffiti the city has to offer, including that of Chris "Freedom" Pape for whom the tunnel is named. His spray-painted rendition of Goya's The Third of May, is lit by sunlight streaming through grates during the waxing and waning hours. No one is recommending that you travel down here (in fact, it's probably illegal), but people do it—mostly in groups, the likes of which you can find by digging through meet-up sites on the Web. Happy spelunking, and may the under-gods go with you.

Moth StorySlams

The city breeds many terrific tales and the Moth bears witness.

Where: Multiple venues (check website)
When: Multiple dates (check website)
Fee: Generally $6–$7 at the door
Website: themoth.org/storyslams

Since truth is stranger than fiction, and the first rule of The Moth StorySlams is that the stories have to be true, you're in for one long, strange evening indeed.

The Moth StorySlams recall bygone eras when sensitive literary types roamed the British countryside or gathered to trade witticisms in bohemian New York salons. The Moth founder George Dawes Green spent many summer evenings on porches in the coastal Carolinas, where he grew up, gathering his friends and spinning yarns (as moths fluttered around the dim porch lights, hence the name). Narratives meandered throughout the night and no one dozed or itched to hit a better party. They sat engrossed in their friends' tales, which gave Green an idea he imported to New York. Green knows it's tough to get people to sit still today, much less to listen.

But The Moth night structure ensures that storytellers capture the audience's attention. Besides being truthful, rules state that stories must last no longer than five minutes, all stories must have a narrative arc, and no notes or rants are allowed. Competition keeps the crowd engaged, too—audience members volunteer to rate the performances and the highest score wins. The rules leave little room for awkward stinkers, but a wide berth for the uncensored human experience.

On each performance night Green provides a theme, like "Beginnings" or "Gifts." Storytellers can tell any story, so long as they adhere, at least loosely, to the theme. The "Beginnings" theme once inspired a story from a Chinese immigrant about her long-held virginal status. She explained how a communist upbringing led to habits that unsettled potential partners, like sleeping motionless on her back, as prescribed by the Chinese government.

Another seasoned Moth storyteller recounted his brutal beating by a group of teens seeking entrance into the Latin Kings, the "beginning" there being the victim's hope that his teen attacker would start a better life upon his release in 15 years. The attack victim won best storyteller, having moved the crowd to tears, but humor prevailed throughout most of the evening. One particularly twisted tale involved a man being followed by a persistent female stalker, whom he later decided to date. She then refused to ever have sex with him, yet the relationship lasted for years.

Once ten winners are chosen over successive evenings, the verbal victors participate in the GrandSLAM SLAMOff. Other Moth events include The Moth Mainstage, which has featured notables such as Margaret Cho, Neil Gaiman and Garrison Keillor; and there is the Gala MothBall, held every November. But the true beauty of The Moth lies in the open StorySlams, where the crowd is forgiving and first-timers can work out their nerves.

You don't have to be famous, published or a keeper of your own blog to take the stage. Regular folks show up at Moth StorySlams with their colorful and crude stories, toss their name into a hat, and get called to deliver. If your story is good, then you can relish the glory of a rapt audience and a possible Moth win. If not, well, back to your cocoon.

Mummified Mother Cabrini

She might be a saint, but this nun could use a divine makeover.

Where: St. Frances Cabrini Shrine, 701 Ft. Washington Ave.
When: Tuesday–Sunday, 9 a.m.–5 p.m.
Phone: 212-923-3536
Getting there: A to 190th St. and Overlook Terrace
Fee: Free

Where do saints go when they die? If you're Mother Frances Xavier Cabrini, a New York nun and the first U.S. citizen to be beatified, you end up in a glass coffin on public display for all eternity.

Thank goodness she's a saint, because if Mother Cabrini were working for the other side this sight would be even creepier than it already is. Sure the chapel's quiet and the soft music is soothing but, seriously, those are human remains lying under the altar, and the wax mask framing her facial skeleton doesn't hide that gruesome fact.

Mother Cabrini first set foot in New York in 1889 to work with immigrants from Italy, her homeland. After dedicating her life to establishing orphanages, schools and hospitals in Europe and the Americas, Mother Cabrini died in 1917, and was canonized in 1946.

Canonization doesn't come easy. The process takes about fifty years and requires that you have two miracles under your belt, fully authenticated by the Roman Catholic Church. Apparently, Mother Cabrini had some influence in restoring the sight of a baby blinded by an accidental overdose of nitrite of silver. After sisters in her church prayed to Cabrini for intercession, the child recovered fully. The second miracle involved another cure, that of a terminally ill nun in Seattle, who had been given only a few days to live. The sister invoked Cabrini's spirit and survived for another twenty years.

Mother Cabrini's transparent coffin is etched with beams of light to indicate her saintly status. The altar is draped in white to symbolize the saint's purity. Her waxen visage gazes up toward the heavens. A wall-mounted showcase and accompanying plaque in the chapel hall give the History of the Remains of Saint Frances Xavier Cabrini with a graphic description of her bodily decay, along with shaved samples of fleshy tissue now reduced to dust. We are told that Mother Cabrini's head and some fingers were severed and sent as relics to her hometown, near Milan, Italy. One of her arm bones resides in Chicago.

It is not unusual for body parts of a saint to be cut up, placed in reliquaries, and used as sacred inspiration, to receive petitions and grant favors anywhere in the world. Her chapel in Upper Manhattan is proud, however, that most of her bones remain entombed there.

According to docents in the shrine's gift shop, the ghost of Mother Cabrini has been spotted on nearby Washington Avenue over the years by many people who have no idea who she is until they step into the chapel and recognize her picture. No worries, though … she's said to be a friendly ghost.

Museum of the American Gangster

Where we learn that organized crime began with our Founding Fathers.

Where: 80 St. Marks Pl., between 1st and 2nd Aves.
When: Check website for hours.
Phone: 800-603-5520
Getting there: 6 to Astor Pl.; R,W to 8th St.
Fee: $10 suggested donation
Website: moagnyc.org

The private alley and secret door are gone, but much of the Prohibition-era memorabilia discovered inside this former speakeasy are still here. So are the personal possessions and paraphernalia of some of the city's most notorious thugs, gangsters, and bootleggers.

The Museum of the American Gangster (MOAG) opened in the spring of 2010 and pays tribute to wise guys throughout our nation's history, with a particular focus on local mobsters like Al Capone and Lucky Luciano, as well as lesser tough guy Walter Sheib. Sheib owned the illegal bar and MOAG building during the later Prohibition years of the 1920s.

The MOAG experience begins in front of the speakeasy's original mahogany bar where museum co-owner and curator Lorcan Otway shares an entertaining history of famous American criminals. Those include, as it turns out, unlikely lawbreakers like John Hancock (molasses smuggler, human trafficker) and Sam Adams (illegal brewer). Otway suggests that the legendary Boston tea party agitators were not protesting a tea tax at all, but rather a sugar tax—sugar to make booze. So began America's bootlegging legacy.

Lorcan is not only MOAG's charismatic owner, but also grew up in the building. His father bought the eastside tenement from Sheib in 1964, and today Lorcan still lives on an upper floor. After his family moved into the building, the Otways realized that Sheib had left behind two large, locked safes in the basement. The elder Otway, too petrified to claim them as his own, called Sheib in Florida to come retrieve their contents. Incredibly, one of the safes contained $2 million in gold currency notes, carefully bundled in newspaper.

Other museum attractions include some period firearms like a Thompson sub-machine gun, vintage whiskey bottles, an old copper still for distilling liquor and newspaper articles that tell the unfolding story of Prohibition gangsters. While it is difficult to engage an audience with faded clippings glued to foam core, Lorcan manages to animate these static displays with his natural charm and a raconteur's verbal deftness.

The tour picks up when you head to the family basement (hiding place of the aforementioned strongboxes), where you'll see a walk-in beer locker, evidence of a steel reinforced "safe room," and wiring for a backbar phone used to alert basement bootleggers of upstairs police raids. A gap in the original stone foundation of this 1840's house reveals a former entrance to a tunnel that ran to 1st Avenue. The underground passage provided both an escape outlet for bootleggers as well as fast access to rum-running speed boats parked in the East River.

The Museum of the American Gangster is a little cheesy, a tad musty, and hardly slick. But for the price of admission, you get to don a cheap hard hat for the stooped walk through the dusty basement where actual human remains have been found. Watch you don't get whacked.

Museum of Sex

Some fetishes titillate and some just disturb.

Where: 233 Fifth Ave. at 27th St.
When: Sunday–Friday, 11 a.m.–6:30 p.m.; Saturday, 11 a.m.–8 p.m.
Phone: 212-689-6337
Getting there: R, W to 28th St. and Broadway; 6 to 28th Street at Park Avenue
Fee: Adults, $14.50; Students and seniors, $13.50
Website: museumofsex.com

The red "X" says you have arrived at the infamous Museum of Sex (MoSex) and from there it is one big salute to the naughty and nasty. From specialty S&M items—including hoods, gags and restraints—to early contraception devices made of everything from wood and glass to metal, MoSex is a shrine to perversion and pleasure.

Porn being mainstream, and this being New York, the museum's presence on lower Fifth Avenue should not be surprising. Pay your admission at

the door and let the leering begin
—at a fascinating collection of kinky
toys, titillating sex machines, sala-
cious video displays and raunchy
works of art.

Vintage sex education material
dating back just a few decades
expresses ideas that now seem
archaic. Visitors gaze in wonder at
antique vibrators, condoms and
rectal dilators, which bring the past
to life in new and unexpected ways.

A fascinating and well-presented
history of straight and queer-
pornography through the ages
begins with early black-and-white
stags and progresses to burlesque,
sexploitation, porn chic and finally,
mainstream and celebrity porn.
Discover why well-known porn
actor Ron Jeremy is called the "hedgehog," step into little side
alcoves with screens that offer a look at racy, surprisingly fleshy European
advertising, and leave believing the French might have actually invented
the tongue.

Visit MoSex on a weekday to avoid the enthusiastic weekend crowds,
although it's always fun to initiate conversations with progressive-minded
tourists, while interacting with a few "hands-on" exhibits. One group of
sultry Italian females slapped themselves into a bondage device on a St.
Andrews cross for photos, and although the signs say "Do Not Touch," a
nearby security guard stared and smiled permissively while leaning against
a cyber S&M full-body suit.

Your museum tour ends by funneling you into the gift and souvenir shop
where you can purchase sex toys, suggestive games, graphic playing cards,
arousing books or unique art pieces. The Italian girls were shopping for
lubricants and bathtub toys.

While this museum might make some happy to have genitals, others may
come away thinking that nothing kills sexiness faster than institutionalizing it.

The National

Boris and Svetlana go out on the town...
and you go with them.

Where: 273 Brighton Beach Ave., Brooklyn
When: Friday, Saturday and Sunday nights; reservations required
Phone: 718-646-1225
Getting there: B, Q to Brighton Beach
Website: come2national.com

An evening at The National restaurant is like crashing your crazy Russian neighbor's wedding. You get many platters of so-so food, tawdry entertainment involving glow-in-the-dark top hats, an endless supply of vodka, and the exuberant Russian drinking songs that go with it. Extended families line long tables topped with white tablecloths and candelabras. Little girls wear princess dresses, and many of the ladies dress—barely—in the latest, scandalous Eastern Euro fashions. Don't come in sneakers and jeans, and don't come tired. The Soviet-style surrealism extends well into the night.

Whether arriving via car or the B or Q lines, your first steps into Brighton Beach require orientation. The beach lies to the south, the rest of the world to the north, and Russia surrounds you. Nicknamed Little Odessa after the city on the Black Sea, the neighborhood halts you at its doorsteps with indecipherable signage, and foreign conversations leave you feeling like a lost traveler. The main thoroughfare, Brighton Beach Avenue, runs forlornly below the elevated subway tracks, retaining little of the bon vivant air of the area's British namesake.

In the midst of the gloom, the sparkling marquee of The National invites you into its gilded interior, spiral staircases wrapping either side of the foyer. A host seated behind an overwrought desk rises to march you to your seats. In the dining room, a burgundy jacquard pattern on the rug is repeated in the fabric wallpaper. Many of the tables are already topped with silver platters piled high with herring, smoked sturgeon and salmon roe. The vodka is flowing before the stage lights go up. The mood is jovial, though maybe not in an Italian "When you're here, you're family!" kind of way.

Soft entertainment begins with the arrival of your main course. Most of the singers (on a recent night there were eight of them onstage) were Russian, except for the one the waiter referred to as "The Big Man." And by big man they mean the looming black singer who croons obscure R&B hits from the early '80s, and who is generally the only non-Russian in the room besides, perhaps, the members of your dinner party. While they may announce the entertainment in Russian, the musical hits hail from the U.S. and Latin America, especially hip-shaking numbers from the crowd favorite, Shakira.

The main event brought the lights down to a complete blackout, until a man jumped onstage and began lip-synching the opening number of *Cabaret*. A gaggle of chorus girls stepped out lit only by their glow-in-the-dark bustiers and top hats with spirals bursting from their crowns. Each number in the medley called for increasingly elaborate black-light accoutrements. Magenta mesh bodysuits were followed by Vegas-style headpieces. If the vodka is treating you right, you can enjoy this kitsch into the wee hours.

A younger generation of Russians is emerging that shuns this local spectacle, so its future is uncertain. But for the time being, you can still get a four-course meal, unlimited vodka and six-plus hours of chintzy entertainment for less than $60. Go early on a summer evening, watch the immigrant cultures brush by each other on the boardwalk, and enjoy the last of the Russian ambiance while it lasts.

SAMMY'S ROUMANIAN STEAK HOUSE
The steak and the schlock without the schlep.

Where: 157 Chrystie St., near Delancey St.
Phone: 212-673-0330
Getting there: J, M, Z to Bowery; F, V to Lower East Side–Second Ave.; B, D to Grand St.

If you don't want to schlep out to Brighton Beach for The National experience, head to Sammy's Roumanian. The food is better, the atmosphere is filled with the same wacky vitality, and it's got that convenient Lower East Side address. Theoretically, you could leave Sammy's and then continue your evening bar hopping in the LES, but it isn't recommended. Here's why.

To start, appetizers include chicken liver served with a syrup bottle full of schmaltz, a.k.a. chicken fat. Or try the Karnatzlack, a sausage of kosher meats drenched in garlic. The Roumanian tenderloin arrives cascading over the edges of the plate. Order it with a tall stack of potato latkes. All the while, the Ketel 1 sits tableside frozen in a block of ice. Tippling is a must if you want to enjoy Danny Luv hacking away at the piano and delivering a heaping side order of vocal schmaltz. He leads the crowd in rousing sing-alongs of such classics as "Sweet Caroline." Conga lines inevitably ensue. A smile already plastered on every patron's face, the wait staff brings the seltzer, chocolate sauce and milk required for unlimited rounds of egg creams.

Now, if you dare to top that off with a Maker's at some LES bar, you'd better keep a bag handy for the taxi ride home. But really, Sammy's, in its fourth decade, housed in a starkly lit, paneled basement, littered with business cards, photos and hokey memorabilia, offers one of the most off-the-wall nights in all of New York. Screw the tony Meatpacking District. This steakhouse delivers the real thing.

New York City Burlesque

Naughty, not creepy.

Where: Venues and reviews mentioned here can be found at
mondaynightburlesque.com, coneyisland.com, slipperroom.com,
lescandal.com, bowerypoetryroom.com, galapagosartspace.com,
wauwausisters.com, pontanisisters.com, misssaturn.com, scottybunny.com
When: Festival happens every fall, see thenewyorkburlesquefestival.com
for details

Watching emcee Scotty the Blue Bunny onstage at the New York Burlesque
Festival, using his metallic purple unitard to make a "puffy pussy" out of
his balls, no one could ever say that NYC had lost its edge. Scotty went
on to tell the audience how he'd come off of Wellbutrin because it made
him puke too quickly, while he was drinking. "So now I can drink more,
so I can do more coke, so I can smoke more weed, so I can suck more
dick." The audience groaned. "Hey, come on, it's New York," he snapped.
Then another burlesque dancer commenced her tease.

Burlesque in New York ain't no Champs Élysée cabaret. The ribald,
slapstick humor of the burlesque and vaudeville circuits stalks the city year-
round. Almost any night of the week, you can find a review: Monday Night
Burlesque at Public Assembly, Burlesque at the Beach at the Coney Island
Sideshow Theater, The Slipper Room's $5 shows every Wednesday
through Saturday night, aerial teases at Galapagos and the Sky Box, or
Le Scandal, which at printing showed every Saturday at the West Bank
Café. You can even catch blood and gore burlesque performances on
occasion at the Bowery Poetry Club.

This post-feminist nouveau-burlesque scene often promotes a body-positive
atmosphere and forces viewers to question what is sexy. The women (and
men!) display acrobatic talent and/or artistic vision. Consider the Wau

Wau Sisters, a comedic acrobat duo that performs feats while hanging above their audience's heads, not hovering over their laps. The popular Pontani Sisters, another mainstay, harken back to old-time burlesque with glittery costumes, shimmies, tap dancing and comedy routines. Miss Saturn, spinning 40 hula hoops at a time, gyrates her way into your heart. The list goes on, excessively so, which brings us to the one draw back: as with any glut, sometimes, you just get a garden-variety stripper.

All of these acts come together once a year at the Burlesque Festival. You can catch the cream of the crop, so to speak, at the main event held on Saturday. Or view a roster of new additions to the scene at the preview night, featuring those still mastering their craft with boas, feather fans, gloves, and pasties as the tools at hand. Even with the monotony of lines of ladies twirling their boobies and grinding their g-strings, there are moments—like when Clams Casino stripped in backlit silhouette, fingerbanged her shadow, and then dribbled some glimmering gold substance down her chin—that make all the tedious titties worthwhile.

JO BOOBS' SCHOOL OF BURLESQUE

Taking it off—the art of striptease for the young and restless.

Where: 440 Lafayette St,, near Astor Pl.
Phone: 212-561-1456
(e-mail preferred: schoolofburlesque@gmail.com)
Website: schoolofburlesque.com

Like any good party, a polished burlesque show makes people want to strip down and join in. But one must not rush the stage until one has mastered the craft. Many a painted lady has honed such skills as popping their fans, peeling off gloves and bedazzling their pasties at Jo Boob's School of Burlesque.

While working for the Burlesque Hall of Fame in Las Vegas, Jo Boobs learned the art of burlesque from dancers who mastered their craft during the '40s and '50s. Those women created an aesthetic that has yet to be surpassed. Boobs, née Jo Weldon, recognized that burlesque movement could and should be taught and opened her school in 2004.

The School holds Burlesque Ballet class every Tuesday with Dirty Martini, and Darlinda and Gal Friday lead the Flirting with Burlesque workout every Thursday. A Sunday series dedicated to essential burlesque movement runs ten months out of the year. Burlesque dancers come from all over the world to teach ladies how to perfect their tease. But more important than knowing how to work boas or whips, or even having a nice rack, burlesque dancer extraordinaire World Famous BOB teaches a class in self-confidence—that essential element of riveting entertainment.

The New York Earth Room

Some sweet city digs for 140 tons of topsoil.

Where: 141 Wooster St., half-block south of Houston St.
When: Wednesday–Sunday, 12–6 p.m. (closed 3–3:30 pm)
Phone: 212-473-8072
Getting there: N, R to Prince St., walk west
Fee: Free
Website: earthroom.org

Shoveling 280,000 pounds of topsoil into a nice apartment would be weird in any city. In New York—where we'll trade non-vital organs for an extra square foot of desirable real estate—it's blasphemous.

A first look at the Earth Room always evokes the same response—WTF! It's simply hard to comprehend why all this inert dirt occupies all this prime loft space, particularly considering how few people pass through to view it. Art apparently justifies the expense. This long-term installation by sculptor Walter De Maria has been lying fallow here since 1977. De Maria says little in the way of explanation, leaving viewers to guess at its purpose: a statement about unchecked development in the city or merely a service to quiet our senses?

An amiable curator, whose demeanor seems as placid as the dirt's, remains on the premises to keep visitors from hopping over the low Plexiglas partition and tiptoeing through the rich black loam. He also harvests the occasional mushroom bloom that grows from floating spores. He claims to use the edible varieties in his salad.

Obscura Antiques

Freakish collectibles, from club-footed shoes to taxidermy rats.

Where: 280 E. 10th St., between 1st Ave. and Avenue A
When: Daily, Noon–8 p.m.
Phone: 212-505-9251
Getting there: 6 to Astor Place
Website: obscuraantiques.com

Right now, someone out there is on a quest for Victorian hair wreaths, strychnine bottles and club-footed shoes. Luckily, Obscura Antiques caters to those demented desires.

This curiosity shop specializes in items with a vaguely ominous presence, like fencing masks, ventriloquist dummies and Masonic memorabilia. Owners Mike Zohn and Evan Michelson hit multiple estate sales every week and constantly replenish their macabre offerings. They maintain a high standard for freakish collectibles. "Some people say, 'Oh, I have weird stuff, too," says Mike, "and then they show you a dentist's mirror." Not happy with just any old medical instrument, Mike says they target the "stuff that makes you afraid to go to the doctor."

Customers in the market for such goods are inevitably impressed by the selection of rare wares here, such as the resin anatomical model baring internal organs for all to ponder. Steampunks can find their Jules Verne goggles here and Goths their taxidermied rats. Prices are high, but affordable, considering the uniqueness of some of these antiques.

Obscura once carried a mummified head that had compartments in the face that swung open. You could feel the stubble on the skin and the texture of the tongue. Mike seemed particularly wistful to have let that one go. His favorite item in the store on a recent visit was a framed photo of a Victorian boy standing with a self-possessed swagger, mounted above a lock of the young dandy's hair.

Whether on an odyssey for stuffed two-headed cow specimens or prosthetic limbs, visitors can fulfill their twisted quests here.

BILLY'S ANTIQUES AND PROP SHOP

The last of the Skid Row flea markets and junk dealers.

Where: 76 E. Houston St. at Elizabeth St.
When: Tuesday–Sunday, 1–8 p.m., weather permitting
Phone: 917-576-6980
Website: billysantiques.com

Once just another circus tent on Skid Row, Billy's Antiques & Props now holds court as a vestige of the area's former low-rent glory. Thanks to a subway grate on the property that supposedly cannot be built on, Billy's is hanging on to its conspicuous spot on Houston St., as the hotels, exclusive boutiques, and high-end antique stores close in.

Billy Leroy, an Upper East Side prep-school boy who went slumming, took over and renamed the canvas-covered, unheated shop in 2003, after the original owner of Lot 76 passed away. This glorified flea market sells horror movie props, curios and reasonably priced vintage furniture (at least by New York standards). An aficionado of the Lower East Side scene, Billy also sells artwork from local artists, such as Paul Richard and Clayton Patterson, of the Clayton Gallery and Outlaw Art Museum (161 Essex Street; gallery shows are often viewable from the street, but tours are available by appointment only; email clayton161@earthlink.net). Billy's clientele includes celebrities and the well groomed, yet the store serves as a neighborhood hangout. Billy sits at the entrance most days with his Rottweiler Kill-Joy at his feet. The staff consists of local characters, and some of the wares come from homeless dumpster divers.

The congenial rogue's gallery serves not only as a junk emporium, but also as a preservation society, making sure at least one corner of Manhattan retains its seedy charm.

Renwick Smallpox Hospital

The island ruins of an imposing hospital for the insane, the diseased and the destitute.

Where: Southern end of Roosevelt Island
Getting there: F to Roosevelt Island; Aerial tram for $2 each way from 59th St. and Second Ave. On the island a red minibus meets the tram and takes you throughout the island for $0.25.
Website: rooseveltislander.blogspot.com

Note: Theoretically, the grounds close at sundown, but the gate sometimes stays open long past dusk. When on the island, also see the Blackwell House, built in 1796 (on the east side of the island, just north of the tram), and the Blackwell Island Lighthouse, at the northern tip of the island.

Few ruins from centuries past remain in New York—real estate is too valuable to let rubble occupy precious space. But the Smallpox Hospital on Roosevelt Island is no ordinary blight. Opened in 1856, this Gothic Revival structure shares its architect with St. Patrick's Cathedral and Grace Church.

A little history for this romantic relic: In 1850, smallpox caused 25.4 out of every 1,000 deaths in New York City. As the epidemic grew, the city looked to Blackwell's Island (as Roosevelt Island was then known), a quarantine for convicts, paupers and the insane. James Renwick, a self-taught architect, designed a symmetrical three-story stone edifice, with a cupola topping the low-pitched hip roof. From 1856 until the 1870s, the hospital housed wealthy patients in private rooms on the upper floor and poor patients in wards on the lower floors. After a scandal uncovered poor conditions, it became a nurse's school, the north and south wings being added in 1905.

After the school closed in the 1950s, the building quickly fell into disrepair. In the '60s, developers began to convert Roosevelt Island (then named Welfare Island) into a residential district. The hospital was granted landmark status in 1975, and everyone spoke of stabilizing the ruins. Yet, besides some lumber supports under the oriels on each wing, the hospital continued to decay. The roof, the floors, and the windows fell away, as the chatter about preservation persisted.

In 1995, the Roosevelt Island Operating Corporation hired the lighting designer for the Statue of Liberty to illuminate the ghostly remains, making it visible at night to drivers on the FDR. While the lights drew attention, they did not bring funding. A *Times* article about fixing the ruins in 1996 described how "the north wall [was] bowed out at the top, perhaps three feet in all." Twelve years later, just as the money for preservation was being appropriated, the north wall finally collapsed in an eruption of bricks and gneiss stone.

Engineers, architects, masons and ironworkers quickly erected scaffolding inside the walls, securing the remaining structure and allowing the ruins to remain picturesque. While the building itself is fenced off, the surrounding park opened to visitors in 2009. Plans are in place to landscape the grounds and develop the site as a space for performances and a seasonal café. At sunset, the lights go up on these romantic stones. To the west, the Chrysler and UN buildings glow from the waning sun. To the north, the Queensboro Bridge casts its latticework silhouette across the skyline. As you stand at the edge of the island, you'll wonder, "Why didn't they think of this sooner?" Followed by, "I wish that café were open. I could sit here all night."

Ripley's Believe It Or Not Odditorium

Crazy impalements, walrus penises, and shrunken heads... enough said.

Where: 234 West 42nd St., between 7th and 8th Aves.
When: 365 days a year, 9 a.m.–1 a.m.
Phone: 212-398-3133
Getting there: A, C, E to 42nd St.
Fee: Adults, $29.95; Children ages 4–12, $24.95
(go to website for 20% online ticket discount)
Website: ripleysnewyork.com

Weird: The stuffed carcasses of a two-headed calf, a six-legged cow, and an albino giraffe, and other "pranks of nature." Weirder: Stunning images of human impalements, including a shocking video of two men riding tandem on a motorcycle, both skewered through the chest by a flying pipe from the back of a suddenly stopping truck (they survived). Weirdest: 24 authentic shrunken heads (the world's largest collection of shriveled noggins), all executed by the Jivaro Indians of Ecuador.

If those entertaining oddities don't bring out the rubbernecker in you, there's 17,000 square feet of equally bizarre attractions at Ripley's, all evoking a constant chorus of "holy shits" from fans of the freakish.

In 1913 a young New York sports cartoonist named Robert LeRoy Ripley started an illustrated feature on the world's most amazing feats and achievements. The subject got under his skin. He spent all his free time circling the world collecting the wackiest and weirdest stuff he could find and opened his first Ripley's Believe It Or Not Museum in New York City in 1939. Known as a place for "curioddities" from over 200 countries, his creation would close and reopen several times over seven decades before finally finding its permanent Times Square home in 2007.

Around every corner here, a reality-defying display proves Ripley's oft-used phrase, "truth can be stranger than fiction." Among the objects: a 2,500-year-old mummified Egyptian hand; the stomach contents of a great white shark (an anchor, shovel, shoes and more); a lock of hair cut from the side of Abraham Lincoln's head near the lethal gunshot wound (strands from Elvis Presley, John F. Kennedy and George Washington are here, too); a four-legged chicken bred by a Romanian farmer eager to yield more drumsticks; a fossilized walrus penis used as a fighting club; and medieval torture devices that make every orifice in your body clench.

It might be tempting to write off Ripley's Odditorium as no more than a lurid collection of freak show memorabilia, a not-worth-the-time tourist trick. Don't make that mistake. Along with plenty of photos of malformed humanity (the astonishing acrobat with no lower body; the world's ugliest woman; an armless man with incredibly dexterous feet), the bulk of the provocative exhibits are thoroughly engaging. Once you make it past the gaudy flashing lights of the Times Square marquis, you're in for an outsized dose of bizarreness. Believe it.

Rossville Marine Graveyard

Dozens of rusting, rotting vessels in a creepy harbor shipyard.

Where: 2453 Arthur Kill Rd., Rossville, Staten Island
When: All the time
Getting there: Visit www.hopstop.com, Google or Mapquest
for detailed directions
Fee: Free

What's creepier than a derelict house, windows boarded up, paint peeling, front steps crumbling? Shipwrecks, that's what. In this case, dozens of gnarled and twisted vessels perilously listing in shallow water, gashes in their rusted hulls offering eerie glimpses into their dark, decaying pasts.

Located in the Arthur Kill tidal strait off the shore of Staten Island, this marine reliquary provides a final resting place for decommissioned and abandoned barges, tugboats, ferries, steamers, and other craft. They ended up in the Arthur Kill because a local salvage company, Donjon Iron and Metal, Inc., was intending to reclaim this sea of floating metal for scrap. But most of ships have been silently rusting here for decades, untouched, taking on brackish water, slowly sinking in the muck.

Not well known and little visited, the marine graveyard has a fascinating beauty, looking as much like an ambitious art installation as an armada run aground. Explore at low tide, when it's easier to access the shoreline and get closer to the boats. But watch out for the swampy paths and bubbling, quicksand-like soil that threatens to suck you into the landscape.

While an easy drive, the bus trip is definitely more of an urban adventure. After transferring from the A train to two bus connections, you'll reach the intersection of Rossville Avenue and Arthur Kill Road. To the right, there is an abandoned cemetery—the Blazing Star Burial Ground. This cemetery, dating from the early 18th century, is filled with chipped and flaking headstones dating as far back as the 1730s, the relentless work of weather and time rendering their etched names almost illegible. A short path leads you through the burial ground to the harbor, where the first hulls come into view, their majestic steel carcasses wrecked and torn.

At the end of the day, visit the Historic Old Bermuda Inn across the street from the burial ground. The ambience of the restaurant, located in a restored Victorian home, reinforces the sense of dark mystery permeating the entire area. The house is said to be haunted by the ghost of a woman who lived there with her husband until he was drafted into Civil War service. He never came back, but she waited in disbelief until the day she died, convinced that he would return. Some dining patrons have felt their hair being stroked, while others have reported seeing a spectral figure lingering on the staircase. Probably waiting around for a ghost ship to come in.

Sailors' Snug Harbor

A former retirement home for the peg-legged and weather-beaten.

Where: 1000 Richmond Terrace, Staten Island
When: Grounds open dawn to dusk; Galleries open
10 a.m.–5 p.m.; Closed Mondays
Phone: 718-425-3524 or 718-425-3586
Getting there: from Manhattan, take the Staten Island Ferry to the
S40 bus to Snug Harbor
Fee: Noble Museum is free; Gallery/garden combo ticket is $6
Website: snug-harbor.org

Seamen historically have been an eccentric, elusive, cantankerous lot— but also, a romantic one. They named their ships after women and spoke of love affairs with the sea. The ocean routinely swallowed their boats whole, maimed fellow sailors and stripped them of their livelihood; these were men intimate with their own vulnerability.

Now, imagine an assemblage of such mariners hobbling about genteel lawns on peg legs, resting on a bench beside a burbling fountain of the god Neptune, or staring out over the industrial Kill van Cull waterway as their former crewmates drift by. That was life at Sailors' Snug Harbor not so many years ago, and the museum complex still carries the gloomy, somewhat doleful air of men's dreams lost at sea.

Snug Harbor, on the northern shore of Staten Island, gave refuge to "aged, decrepit, and worn out sailors" throughout the 19th and much of the 20th centuries. A bequest of Robert Richard Randall, it was once New York's richest philanthropy. Its buildings, built in the Greek Revival, Beaux

Arts, and Italianate styles, speak to this wealth. The environment looks more like a slightly decayed noble court than housing for a neglected population.

In one of the Greek Revival-style dormitory buildings, the Noble Maritime Museum displays a collection of John Noble's artwork. Noble (b. 1913; d. 1983), the son of an artist, fell in love with the working vessels of the Harbor and worked for many years in marine salvage. His seventy-nine lithographs detail the danger and isolation of life on tugs and ships. Through Nobel's artwork, we learn just how vicious the weather off New York's shores can be, how storm-tossed tugs used to yank massive ships through offshore waves, and how often these vessels never made it to safe harbor. In 1941, Nobel built a houseboat studio out of other ships and moored it in the Port Johnston coal yard, which had become the world's largest graveyard of wooden sailing ships. He traveled the rivers of New York in a rowboat and recorded the city's maritime history. The Museum also holds this houseboat studio, arranged as though Nobel might return from the ship's head and surprise you at any moment.

The Museum also contains a recreation of a typical dormitory room. Other rooms contain artifacts such as wicker wheelchairs that might have held an ailing salty dog. After you've absorbed the sights here, head next door to the Visitor's Center in the Main Hall. Its painted ceiling arches up to a domed glass cupola with a compass and weather vane in the center. A display outlines the history of Snug Harbor, from the first blind, one-legged and "lame" sailors who inhabited this place to the last to leave (shipped down to North Carolina in 1972).

Today, Snug Harbor has been recast as a cultural center, with the Staten Island Children's Museum and various gardens, galleries and performance spaces located throughout the 83 acres. But several of the buildings remain un-restored. Standing on the columned steps of the dormitories, gazing through cherry blossoms and shade trees, over the shorefront road, out to the tugs on Kill van Cull, with the tankers of Bayonne on the distant shore, you'll feel the sailors' mournful presence. What longing, and what loneliness.

Spa Castle

A theme park for cleanliness (and that includes your butt crack).

Where: 131-10 11th Ave., College Point, Queens
When: Daily, 6 a.m.–Midnight
Phone: 718-939-6300
Getting there: 7 to last stop, get Spa Castle Shuttle from there
Fee: Varies with services
Website: nyspacastle.com

Anyone who has ever stepped over a city gutter, used the bathrooms in Penn Station or grabbed a subway handrail knows this for a fact: nothing in New York City is clean. Soot and grime and litter and gum sully every surface but the Great Lawn. What a relief, then, to step through the doors of Spa Castle, to eye its sleek interior, and to pad your bare feet across its pristine floors. Let the cleansing begin!

Spa Castle (located next to an industrial park in Queens) replicates the Korean jimjilbang—futuristic spa theme parks the whole family can enjoy. Guests get a Swatch-looking fob that opens your locker (with a digitized flourish) and tallies your tab. In gender-segregated dressing rooms, shoes are immediately placed in a tidy, tiny locker and the rest of your clothing in a separate compartment. Then, you plod your bare butt into the mandatory naked room and commence the scouring of every crevice.

Dimly lit, with dark stone walls, the naked room contains showers, four hot baths, a massage jet pool, cool and cold splash pools, and wet and dry saunas. No staff member speaks English and a majority of guests are Korean, Japanese or Eastern European. So, Americans tend to fumble their way through the experience. But your first step in proper spa procedure is to lose that awkward shyness. Yes, you just saw some grandma's nether regions, but you'll live.

Next, wash yourself—well. Get in your butt crack, wash your hair to the root, and then thoroughly rinse. Brush your teeth with the toothbrush they give you. Then, climb into the hot baths. Soak for 10 minutes, and then hit the cold water for a few. Lounge in the massage pools, followed by the cold water. Wet sauna, cold water. Dry sauna, cold water. With skin tenderized, female guests begin an exfoliation ritual, which takes place on low stools in front of lit mirrors. Using special gloves (available for $2 at the desk), you start to scrub off layers of dead skin cells. Feeling good about their supple, glowing skin, all guests don a prison-issue shorts ensemble to wear to the three unisex floors.

The next floor houses a food court (get the bibimbop, skip the sushi), lines of massage chairs, a heated floor for napping and seven themed saunas arranged in a pod village. If short on time, skip the gold, the color-therapy and the infrared saunas. Instead, relax while surrounded by the sparkling geodes of the jade sauna or the pink salt blocks of the salt sauna, and then swelter in the 190-degree heat of the Loess soil room, intermittently freezing in the Iceland cold sauna. A recommendation: after eating, start with the cooler saunas and work your way up the thermometer.

Bring your bathing suit and towel to the third floor, where you'll wade in heated indoor and outdoor pools filled with massage jets and overhead waterfalls. Finally, wrap up the day with another shower. The best times to go are weekdays or late nights during the school year, when you'll avoid the crowds (and the kids). Leave anytime before rush hour, which would surely ruin your groovy mood. And until you get home, don't touch anything.

Passing Peculiarity

PRIVATE PASSAGE

WHERE: CLINTON COVE, 55TH ST. AND 12TH AVE.

Oh, look, a nice sized NYC apartment…in a bottle. A tipped-over wine bottle, in fact, and the clever creation of artist Malcolm Cochran that he calls *Private Passage*. As a kid, Cochran once traveled to Europe on an ocean liner. That experience, and the fact that the west side of Manhattan has always been a departure point for luxury cruise ships, prompted him to forge a stateroom out of polished sheet metal (reminiscent of those on the RMS Queen Mary), and place it inside a 30' x 8'6" bronze and zinc bottle, treated to a green patina. Portholes along the sculpture's side, and rounded windows on both ends, permit distorted views of the interior, outfitted with metal toilet, bed and lounge chair. The message in the bottle? Art is cool but you wouldn't want to nap in it.

ONLY IN NEW YORK STORIES 3

I LEFT A MOVIE THEATER ON EAST 59TH STREET AFTER SEEING "KISS OF THE SPIDER WOMAN" WITH TWO CALIFORNIA FRIENDS. WE WERE TRYING TO GET A TAXI AT THE END OF A SHIFT WHEN THE CABBIES WERE HEADING HOME. THE TWO DRIVERS WE HAILED SAID, "QUEENS ONLY." THE FEMALE CALIFORNIAN WAS INDIGNANT. SHE LOOKED AT ME AND SAID, "I'VE NEVER HEARD OF SUCH A THING! THEY WON'T TAKE STRAIGHT PEOPLE?!"

— DIANA LAGUARDIA

All that stood between me and the subway station was the methadone treatment center and its loudest homeless patient—call him Daniel. Every day I crossed the street to avoid running into him on my way to work; every day my husband gave Daniel a few dollars on his way to the station. One day my husband and I walked by Daniel together. He looked up from the street, stared my husband in the eye and said, "She is such a bitch." We moved to a different apartment.

— MONIKA JAIN

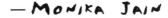

When working at a magazine downtown I went to deliver a $500 cash payment to a vendor in Sheridan Square, and stopped in a phone booth to make a call. When I got to the vendor I realized I had left the envelope in the phone booth. My boss was furious. Until two days later when he received a call from a long-lost, down-and-out friend. Desperate for money, this man had been checking for coins in public phones and coincidentally found the envelope stuffed with cash. It had my boss's return address on it and the man was calling to thank my boss, his old friend, for saving his life.

— DL

In spring 2005, exiting the subway, I had too many packages and asked the token booth collector to open the gate for me. He refused, insisting I use the turnstile. I asked again. He refused again. I approached the token booth and asked for his badge number to report him. Someone behind me said, "What's the problem?" I started speaking before I turned around, saying, "He wouldn't open the door for me"... I was shocked to be complaining to Alec Baldwin who then put one hand on the token booth glass and the other on my shoulder and said, "Can't we all just get along on Martin Luther King's Day?"

— CAROL ASCH

I had just gotten taken by those 5-Card Monte swindlers on Broadway. As they ran off, I started crying hysterically, stomping my feet, and yelling at them and anyone else who would listen to me. After a short time, I started walking away. I was then approached by another guy a few blocks later who told me to follow him down a side street. I courageously (or stupidly) walked with him to a side alley and there I met the swindler who gave me my money back and hugged me.

— JO DiMAURO

Surfing at Rockaway Beach

Wax up, folks, there's radical wave riding at the distant end of the subway line.

New York Surf School
Phone: 718-496-3371
Website: surflessonsnewyork101.com

Boarders Surf Shop
Where: 192 Beach 92nd. St., Queens
Phone: 718-318-7997
Website: boarderssurfshop.com

Rockaway Beach does not evoke scenes from *The Endless Summer* or *Riding Giants*. There is no tropical paradise here, and no amount of squinting can erase the housing projects or the abandoned bungalows crawling with feral cats. Yet, the cross streets do end at a beach with a sand bottom beach break that delivers good waves. And that's all a surfer needs.

In 1912, Duke Kahanamoku of Hawaii, the father of modern surfing, demonstrated the sport to a rapt audience in Rockaway Beach. New Yorkers, being the trendy types that they were (and are), quickly took to wave riding, and the Rockaway surf scene was born. While most natives have heard of surfing within the five boroughs, few have actually seen or done it. Over the years, Rockaway surfers have earned a reputation for toughness. It takes a special level of dedication to drag surfboards down from 5-story walk-ups and onto crowded trains, only to paddle out into 50-degree water in the middle of November on a stretch of beach where pilings lurk submerged at high tide. The view of the shore looks almost desolate, with the Manhattan skyline rising like a jagged crown. There is no enjoying the discordant scenery—there are only the waves.

From Memorial Day to Labor Day, Beach 90th Street to Beach 92nd Street is a dedicated surfing beach, with all beaches open the rest of the year. Most often, breakers range from one to three feet, but hurricanes will stir up 7-foot crests, making the locals giddy as storms move up the coast. Currently, three surf shops serve the surf community, Rockaway Beach Surf Shop, Boarders and FTW, which is run by Bobby Vaughn, a SoCal surfer and co-founder of Von Dutch. Vaughn felt Rockaway needed high-performance boards and as he put it in a *New York Magazine* article, "to embrace its inner gangster." But the waves mostly require long boards, and Rockaway prides itself on its unpretentious lack of style. As Frank Cullen, director of the New York Surf School put it, "It's just a nice, friendly scene." You'll get territorial locals anywhere, he says, but if you don't show up and act like a jackass, you shouldn't have a problem.

The scene continues to grow. Kids are moving out from Williamsburg and the LES, in search of the ramshackle romanticism of an urban coastline. Daytrippers can hit up the New York Surf School for lessons. The school provides the wetsuits and surfboards, and Boarders provides lockers, changing rooms and hot showers.

In all fairness, many sections of Rockaway feel like any little beach town anywhere in the world. Except it's not anywhere in the world. It's at the end of the A train. In Queens.

Thoth

Where would NYC be without a Thoth "prayformance"?

Where: Angel Tunnel at Bethesda Fountain in Central Park
Website: skthoth.com

When confronted with the truly unique, our brains struggle to categorize it. The mental strain and confusion can lead to slack jaw, giggles or confounded shakes of the head. Or, in the case of an America's Got Talent audience as it witnessed a Thoth "prayformance," many expressed themselves by booing, loudly. David Hasselhoff hopped around clutching his belly and Piers Morgan sneered, while Sharon Osborne, no stranger to the strange, watched and smiled. Despite approval from Osborne, there would be no million dollars for Thoth.

In short, Thoth is a freaky street performer who does "prayformances" of his "solopera" about a hermaphrodite kid in a made-up kingdom where Thoth has basically been living in his mind all his life. But there is more to this man. Thoth is a concert-level violinist and a true counter-tenor. His mother, a timpanist, became the first black musician to play with the New York Philharmonic. She and Thoth's father, a white Jewish doctor, were communists committed to civil rights and creating a more tolerant world for their mixed-race children.

Then, reality struck. Thoth, née Stephen Kaufman, endured racist taunts throughout his childhood. His parents eventually divorced, his father disappeared from his life, and young Stephen retreated into his overwrought imagination. Emotionally repressed and deep in an identity crisis,

Stephen failed at a suicide attempt in his early 20s but subsequently found his voice.

Thoth, who was once acutely self-conscious, also found his body and put it in motion and on display. Dressed in a loincloth, some chains and a headdress, he unleashes his inner turmoil through arresting performance art. In a made-up language, he sings the tale of the hermaphrodite Nuvarin in the land of Festad. Wearing heavy-heeled shoes and bells on his ankles, Thoth pounds out rhythms while singing, dancing and playing the violin. The music resonates through the Angel Tunnel at Bethesda Fountain, and the effect is transcendent. The gathered crowd stands mute. No one snickers. Without understanding his words or knowing the story, the audience of passersby understands the depth of emotion that has just been laid bare.

Thoth, now over 50, has performed around the world and was the subject of an Oscar-winning documentary, *Thoth*. He comes off as charming, intelligent and mildly crazy. He may seamlessly segue from a story about himself into speaking from Nuvarin's perspective. He admits that he blurs the line between reality and fantasy. When asked, as he often is, about how he makes enough money to live, he expresses anxiety at his situation. Yet, he professes a deep belief that love moves the world more than money. In a quote you'll want to keep in your back pocket for trying financial times, he says, "I'm just sitting up here in my love tree and I'm saying, Hey, don't chop me down with your money axes."

---

346 Broadway Tower Clock

Off-limits for years, now you can climb inside this fabled timepiece.

Where: Enter at 108 Leonard St., between Broadway and Lafayette Sts.
When: Weekdays, by appointment
Phone: Call Forest Markowitz at 212-788-3525
Getting there: A, C, E to Canal St.; B, D, F, V to Broadway–Lafayette St.
Fee: Free

Essentially closed since 9/11, the hidden clock tower at the 346 Broadway building is officially a New York City historic landmark. And historic landmarks must be accessible to the public to keep their esteemed status. That means anyone can climb to the top to see the majestic clock, its 5,000-pound bronze bell and the inner workings of its amazing machinery.

The escapade starts when you call the bowtie-clad Forest Markowitz, a longtime city employee and amiable guide, who has become the building's de facto clock master (and who holds the keys). He will arrange a time for you to meet him in the lobby of the city-owned building, at which time you will pass through airport-like security, take an elevator to the 12th floor, and walk a maze of hallways until your reach the tower base. Forest pulls out the key that unlocks the door that takes you to a spiral staircase that leads you to this crazy beautiful ancient clock.

Forest regales you with fascinating details about this notable tower and its original machinery. The building is an 1898 Stanford White architectural masterpiece, capped with a clock tower that houses the city's largest mechanical clock—meaning it works purely by weights and pendulums, not electricity.

Built by the renowned Boston-based Howard Clock Company, it's a #4 striking style clock, one of only four left in the world (its famous sister lives in Chicago's Wrigley Building).

The clockworks are enclosed in a glass machinery room and require more than a dozen gears, ranging in size from a half inch wide to a full two feet, to drive the mechanisms that turn the enormous clock hands. Those hands stand against a Roman numeral dial in four massive windows. When it hits the hour, hold your ears, as the hammer slams into a cast bronze bell twice the size of the Liberty Bell. Fifteen feet above at the peak of the tower, two of four Tiffany skylights remain.

Allow a solid hour for Forest to tell you about the spurned lover who snuck up to the tower in 1912 to hang himself from the spiral staircase banister. His ghost has dibs on the place apparently (visitors claim they've felt breathing on their necks and a presence in their midst). Erotic scenes from the 1986 drama 9½ Weeks were also shot up here. Forest will show you exactly where Mickey Rourke and Kim Bassinger used the clock tower for...well...just about everything. There's also the case of the mysterious disappearing statue that rested atop the tower—four Atlas figures shouldering a globe with an eagle at its apex. The 30-ft. high metal sculpture more or less vanished from the roof in 1950, and Forest thinks he might have tracked it down to a farm in upstate New York. Ask him for an update. You might also be lucky enough to see him wind the clock, something Forest must climb up here to do every seven days to keep the time chiming.

Unfortunately, surrounding building construction has obscured the historic tower from street view, although you can catch a glimpse of it from the south on Broadway. Best to simply set some time aside to meet with this anecdote-filled clock master and take the trek to the tower's top.

You'll earn this one.

Toy Tokyo

Some toys aren't meant to be shared.

Where: 121 2nd Ave., 2F, between 7th and 8th Sts.
When: Daily, 1–9 p.m
Phone: 973-759-0200
Getting there: 6 to Astor Place; F to Second Ave.
Website: toytokyo.com

Members of the Boomer to Gen Y set enjoy worshiping at the altar of frivolity. Only we would consider a G.I. Joe action figure to be an investment. Only we continue to feel the tension of watching another child play with our limited-edition Simpsons Treehouse of Horrors conversational set. That Millennium Falcon our parents denied us? It's ours now, you cheapskates.

With customers this intense in mind, Toy Tokyo offers a copious yet meticulous selection crammed into a second-floor apartment in the East Village. A die-cut Godzilla used to guard the graffitied doorway; now, there's just a sidewalk sign. Up the narrow, puckered stairway, past the toy dispensers full of Japanese miniatures, you enter an oasis of quirky imagination. To the left, you see a wall of blind boxes (i.e. your purchase is a surprise), including the Rements miniature sushis. Round the corner to the Steamboat Willie figurines, vintage promotional toys and Nightmare before Christmas dolls. What's this? Why it's a Yoda knapsack. Ooh! Rizzo the Rat preserved in PVC! Mosey onto another aisle and find an array of tin wind-up robots, with a '50s comic-book appeal. Stikfa pose-able warriors line more shelves (they're awesome, by the way), across from those, an assortment of Godzilla monsters.

Hardcore collectors should head directly to the back of the store. Deep pockets can get you a Ron English Fat Ronald McDonald, a KAWS Kubrick or a limited-edition Michael Lau vinyl, each of which fetches about $200. A trip to Toy Tokyo is like perusing the Sears catalogue right before Christmas. But now, if your bills are paid or your credit line is long enough, you don't have to ask Santa and you don't have to wait. Ah, adulthood.

Troma Studio Tour

Free peek into the shameless, tasteless world of B-movie making.

Where: 36-40 11th Street, Long Island City
When: Monday–Friday, 12–6 p.m., by appointment
Phone: 718-391-0110
Getting there: F train to 21st St./Queensbridge, walk east then south
Fee: Free
Website: troma.com

If you've ever seen the Toxic Avenger films, you already know the work of Troma Entertainment. This maker of low budget horror comedies, laden with eroticism, gratuitous violence and crude humor, claims to be the oldest, fully independent movie studio in the world. Troma, along with its creator Lloyd Kaufman, has had a significant impact on today's youth culture and influenced some highly regarded filmmakers and actors.

Since 1974, Troma has produced more than 1,000 feature films, the four Toxic Avenger movies being the best known and spawning a popular children's cartoon show in the early 1990's called "The Toxic Crusaders." Over the years, Troma-produced films have given starts to actors like Marisa Tomei, Kevin Costner, Samuel L. Jackson, David Straithairn and Vincent D'Onofrio. Troma was also the first to recognize the work of humorists Matt Stone and Trey Parker in 1996 with the release of "Cannibal! The Musical," a couple years before the two launched their mega-successful South Park franchise.

Even more impressive is the roster of Troma fans who became prominent filmmakers themselves and cite the studio's edgy, sometimes awful work as shaping their own cinematic visions: Peter Jackson, Quentin Tarantino, Guillermo Del Toro and Spain's Alex de la Iglesia.

The nerve center for the self-proclaimed "world's greatest concentration of camp" sits in a crummy non-descript building in an industrial area of Long Island City (there is no actual movie studio here, just a spacious vault for original film reels, a basement filled with cool props, digital editing equipment and lots of eager interns). The free tour is short—just 20 minutes long—but for die-hard fans, Troma is a Mecca. And when he's in town, the always entertaining Lloyd Kaufman (who possesses a striking resemblance to comedian Mel Brooks) might pop out to speak with visitors about his "tromatic" film career and what he calls his "cellu-Lloyd" masterpieces. His office alone is worth the trip to LIC—it's looks like every noxious character in his raunchy films puked up their guts on his desktop.

If you are a student of motion pictures and are interested in getting valuable exposure to the world of independent filmmaking and distribution, speak to your "tour guide" about interning at Troma. A bustling environment that's making innovative use of new cinematic and digital technologies, Troma would be delighted to exploit your creative services while occasionally making you don the "Toxie" mask to frighten tour guests.

And here's an interesting aside. The wife of Troma's founder and chief schlockmeister is none other than Patricia Kaufman—the New York State Film Commissioner.

Vertical Tour of St. John the Divine

If you want to get closer to God, start climbing.

Where: 1047 Amsterdam Ave., between 110th and 112th Sts.
When: Every Saturday at Noon and 2 p.m.
Phone: 212-316-7490
Getting there: 1 to Cathedral Pkwy./110th St.; B, C to 110th St./
Cathedral Pkwy.
Fee: $15 (Call to reserve at 866-811-4111 or via website)
Website: stjohndivine.org

The enormous Cathedral of St. John the Divine, barely more than a century old, was conceived in the medieval tradition. During construction, the designers assigned the finest craftsmen to work at the cathedral's heights, the theory being that God lives in Heaven, and he's particularly focused on the cathedral's soaring spires and peaks. By extension, if you want to hobnob with the Almighty, start climbing.

The popular Vertical Tour of St. John the Divine is offered twice a day, every Saturday, but the large number of visitors does not undermine its drama or appeal. Whether you find yourself on the tour with hipsters or aging nerds, the ascent through the architecture of one of the largest cathedrals in the world offers a surprise at every turn.

The tour starts on the floor of the cavernous nave. You stare up at the ribbed archways of the ceilings, as the Gothic clusters of columns disappear into the upper shadows. You wonder how a structure made of granite, brick, mortar and limestone can feel so warm and welcoming. Perhaps the mystery lies in the geometry, with all the cathedral's measurements incorporating the sacred number seven. Consider these stats: the height of the nave is 124 feet (1 plus 2 plus 4 equals 7). The width of the nave: 124 feet. The circumference of the stained-glass Rose Window, the largest in the U.S.: 124 feet. The length of the nave: 601 feet (do the math). Is the Almighty at play in every measured step?

The buttresses bear all of the cathedral's weight and allow for massive stained-glass windows. Each bay features a series of windows dedicated to various professions. You start your climb through an unmarked door between the Medical and Communications bays. The first expanse of glass in the Communications bay features such achievements as the linotype and the printing press. Created in the 1930s, the window also predicts the invention and importance of television. The cathedral's glorification of the contributions of laymen seems to empower visitors—atheist, agnostic and religious alike.

Next, you climb through a dark spiral staircase, lighting your steps with flashlights. On the triforium level are the carved rosettes on the column capitals, intense stonework that few would see if not for this tour. Rooms once reserved for artists-in-residence line this level. On the Rose level, a large stone rose carving frames the view. From here, you momentarily step out onto the roof for a birds-eye look at Morningside Heights. Then the tour climbs higher still to a point above the cathedral ceiling. You duck through a door and enter "La Foret," the forest, the timber interior of the roof. The vaults of each archway lurch up and over, up and over, into the dark distance. Here, you can experience the heady excitement of a child who has stumbled upon a magical attic.

St. John the Divine conducts unusual masses and opens its doors for unconventional gatherings, the Procession of the Ghouls (see page 123) and the Blessing of the Animals (see page 113) among them. It is a living cathedral, as imperfect as any of us, an idiosyncratic work in progress. If you want to understand its relevance to New York, be sure to make this vertical visit. As one visitor exclaimed, "This is the coolest tour I've ever taken."

THE PEACE FOUNTAIN   Where: St. John the Divine (see previous page)

With all due respect to the church, this sculpture is f***ed up.

On your way out of the big cathedral, stop to gawk at the perplexing Peace Fountain on the church's Great Lawn. Commissioned in 1985, this cast-bronze sculpture lords over the garden at 40 feet tall and weighing 16 tons. While it no longer holds water, the fountain streams used to cascade down various chutes into a tumultuous whirlpool at the bottom.

Symbolizing the triumph of good over evil, the Archangel Michael looms over the body of a decapitated Satan. Hung from its protruding arteries, Satan's head dangles gruesomely from a crab claw. A double helix of DNA, the key to life, runs up the side of the pedestal. Nine giraffes nuzzle St. Michael, while the moon and sun emit tranquility and joy. Cast animal sculptures from primary grade students ring the edges of the fountain, giving viewers ample subject matter to stew on and discuss.

Completely unorthodox, the Peace Fountain serves as a fitting sidekick to the quirky St. John the Divine, melding religion, spirituality and science seamlessly in one finite, if somewhat overbearing, space. If you're lucky, the church's peacocks will strut out for a visit in the adjacent garden, and if you look way up, Quasimodo might peek out from the flying buttresses. It would only be fitting.

Village Chess Shop and Chess Forum

Join the clash of ivory armies on an otherwise peaceful Village street.

Village Chess Shop:
Where: 230 Thompson St., between
W. 3rd and Bleecker Sts.
When: Daily, 24 hours
Phone: 212-475-9580
Getting there: A, C, E, F, V to
West 4th St.
Website: chess-shop.com

Chess Forum:
Where: 219 Thompson St., between
W. 3rd and Bleecker Sts.
When: Daily, 10 a.m.–12 a.m.
Phone: 212-475-2369
Getting there: A, C, E, F, V to
West 4th St.
Website: chessforum.com

Chess players seem to live their whole lives at war, constantly strategizing, dissecting weaknesses, arguing over whether an opponent's move was somehow dishonorable. As such, it hardly seemed fitting for the Village Chess Shop to have once lacked a competitor. The opening of the Chess Forum in 1995 sparked a bitter rivalry not seen since the Cold War.

According to legend, the skirmishes date back to the '60s, when George Frohlinde worked at the chess shop of Russian grandmaster Nicholas Rossolimo. For several years, Frohlinde ran the shop while Rossolimo went abroad, until a dispute broke out over money. So, in 1972 Frohlinde opened the Village Chess Shop. Meanwhile, Rossolimo returned to revive his own shop, fell down some stairs and died. His shop closed.

Following Bobby Fischer's defeat of Boris Spassky in 1972, dozens of chess shops opened up, only to close within a few years. By 1987, the Village Chess Shop was the only game in town. Frohlinde was getting old and started negotiating with employee Imad Khachchan to take over the store. Those talks fell through, and Khachchan opened Chess Forum almost directly across the street. Mayhem broke out. Lawsuits were flying, price wars were raging, customers were forced to sign loyalty oaths, and traitors were banned from both shops. The feud raged for more than a decade.

In recent years, an uneasy truce has been reached. Customers at both shops meander from one to the other to meet friends. Each shop feels well worn, ramshackle, in need of a coat of paint and a good scrubbing. Customers fill the lines of tables, either playing or watching other people play. Heated matches of speed chess go on, hands flying between pieces and the clock, pieces flying off the table, mouths talking a mild amount of trash. Old-timers welcome newcomers with a barrage of instruction. They refer to games played by José Raul Capablanca and Emanuel Laskar. Players from the highest levels of chess frequent these two holdouts, like William Lombardi, who served as Bobby Fischer's second at the world chess championship in 1972. Chess Forum attracts a slightly younger crowd, while the Village Chess Shop gathers a dustier set.

At both, it costs $3/hour to watch, $2/hour to play (hovering is discouraged). Anyone is welcome, but it's best to arrive armed with some knowledge of the game. And, remember, chess is war. Your match might be friendly, but it is never benign.

CHESS HUSTLERS OF NEW YORK CITY

Chess. Speed. Scenery. Checkmate.

Where: West side of Union Square; Southwest corner of Washington Square Park; Next to the fountain terrace on 6th Ave. in Bryant Park; Chess and Checkers House, Central Park and 65th St., west of The Dairy
When: Good weather (i.e. spring through fall when it isn't raining)

Chess hardly seems a royal game when played on these mean city streets. Ubiquitous as handball or streetball, the playing of chess blends into the scenery of New York. In Bryant Park, Washington Square Park or Union Square, the games may stand as a calm center among the squawking of performers and blur of pedestrians. Other times, the trash-talking hustlers become the spectacle itself.

Many chess hustlers, a scruffy lot, play at the master level. Often former tournament players, their trade is less hustle than service. They bring the chess pieces, the board and their game. You pay for the convenience and the challenge; unless, of course, you're better than they are. Usually, games cost $3 each, although it's not unheard of for gambling to enter the fray. During a heated match of speed chess, pieces sail off the table in all directions amid a flurry of flailing arms. Harmless spats may arise over choices of strategy, but the hustlers rarely seek to rip people off. They need return customers. Most days the mood is laid back, and the comers hardly expect to win. They're there to gain experience. If they lose some money, well, then lesson learned.

Water Taxi Beach

Cement, cement, cement,...sand!

Where: North Side of Pier 17, Fulton and South Sts.
When: 2 p.m.–4 p.m, May through October, except Monday and Tuesday
Phone: 877-974-6998, ext. 4
Fee: Free to frolic
Website: watertaxibeach.com

Down by the South Street Seaport they've put a sandy crack in the hard crust of Manhattan Island cement. It's basically a big sandbox (437 tons of sand spread over 22,000 square feet of riverfront space) with a bar and admittedly far fewer freaks than you'd see in Venice Beach. There are even some families with kids. You can sunbathe under kitschy plastic palm trees, with bust-out views of the Brooklyn and Manhattan Bridges.

Don't even think about going in the water (the currents here will suck you down—for real—plus it's illegal), but if you'd like to spread a blanket or sarong for a couple of hours, have an umbrella drink or local beer, and enjoy some unforgettable people-watching (after sunset it caters to a 21+ crowd for music and tippling), this sandbar gets high marks.

There's another trucked-in beach in Long Island City that's twice the size, plus a new one on Governor's Island that is more of a music destination, but the South Street Seaport's pocket beach looks the most out of place, which makes it the most fun for boozy sandcastles and sunny fun.

Whispering Gallery

Why are those people talking to that wall?

Where: Grand Central Station at 42nd St., outside of the Oyster Bar Restaurant

It can be hard to find sweet and innocent moments in this wild and scruffy city. But at the Whispering Gallery in Grand Central Station, they happen all the time.

Just outside the Oyster Bar Restaurant, three corridors merge under a Guastavino tiled archway (more than 300 examples of Rafael Guastavino's work exists throughout NYC, including in the City Hall Subway Station, see page 24, and on the ceiling of St. John the Divine, page 103). At any given time, passersby may notice individuals standing with their noses in a corner of the crossing. Unbeknownst to many, they're engaged in a secret exchange. The curved hard surface creates a perfect conductor of sound from one diagonal corner of the archway to the other. As the rush of commuters breezes under the low vaulted ceiling, two people may be sharing sweet-nothings overhead, or dirty jokes, or even marriage proposals. In fact, rumor has it Charlie Parker popped the question here. The phenomenon repeats inside the Oyster Bar Restaurant, where patrons at one table may hear another party's conversation perfectly across the crowded room.

A surprising number of New Yorkers still don't know about this little bit of whimsy. And no matter how well prepared or expectant you are, the moment when a friend or loved one's voice comes cascading down to your piqued ear never ceases to elicit a giggle. You'll whip your head around to confirm that the deliverer is still standing 40 feet away. See? Magic!

Wildman Steve Brill Tours

Tripping through the daisies to pick some wild mushrooms.

Where: Throughout the tri-state area
When: Frequently; check the website schedule and reserve your spot.
Phone: 914-835-2135
Website: wildmanstevebrill.com

Many New Yorkers long to wander through the woods, yet the idea also petrifies them. Could there be poison ivy, noxious mushrooms or, you know, rabid squirrels? For these people, Wildman Steve Brill is an urban Daniel Boone, providing safety and reassurance. An author and environmental educator with a lengthy resume, Brill knows his juneberries from his black nightshade (neither of whose berries are poisonous, but the leaves of nightshade can be deadly).

For more than two decades, this freak of nature has been hosting foraging tours through public green spaces in the tri-state area. But the idea of picking edible plants in the wilds of New York City runs counter to all conventional wisdom. In fact, it so threw the NYC Parks Department that when it learned of a crazy man eating dandelions in the park—and encouraging others to do the same—they performed a sting operation to arrest him. Surely, this can't be legal, they decided. But Brill turned his subsequent court date into a public spectacle, selling wild greens on the courthouse steps. The press ate it up. Soon he found himself on David Letterman and other TV shows, the city newspapers following every turn in the case. After much wrangling, his tours were not only allowed, but also sanctioned by the parks department.

One recent four-hour tour, with kids and adults of all ages in attendance, started on 103rd St. and Central Park West. Brill can be a bit brusque, calling no-shows on his cell phone to determine first if they were lost and then to chastise them for bailing. A recent group ventured out by heading north, then quickly lost all bearings and meandered in every direction, with the Wildman occasionally turning people on their heels when he realized he'd missed a good path for mushrooms or sassafras.

Brill stumbled across the white flowers of a snakeroot plant and the group learned that when cows eat it, it creates toxic milk, the cause of death for Abraham Lincoln's mother. He also discovered epazote, difficult to find fresh in grocery stores but available in abundance throughout Central Park. You can use it in small doses in Mexican bean dishes or mole. There are medicinal uses for park plants, too, like jewelweed (rub it on a poison ivy exposure) and common plantae (mash it up and apply it to mosquito bites), which Brill's precocious four-year-old daughter identified on her own. The group also harvested edible mushrooms to bring home, including hen-of-the-forest and chicken mushrooms, for which Brill provided recipes.

In this paved-over city, a Wildman tour is a refreshing experience. It reassures us that the earth is, in fact, beneath our feet. And when the group rounded the bend at the end of the tour and marched, children in tow, through the Polyamorous Society's gathering on the North Meadow, all were reminded that, yes, this is definitely still New York.

i Pak Spa

Good skin…with just a hint of torture.

Where: 10 W. 32nd St., 2nd Fl., near 5th Ave.
When: Daily, 8 a.m.–12 p.m.
Phone: 212-564-8882
Getting there: N, R, Q, W, B, D, F, V to 34th St.
Website: yipakspa.com

If you've ever fantasized about being slapped around like a piece of meat by a couple of elderly Korean women dressed in black bras and panties, then Yi Pak is your spa. Bereft of New Age music, flower petals, aromatherapy or any of that crap, this spa delivers one thing and one thing only: good skin. To get there, you spill off 32nd St. into a dull, narrow lobby, climb the yellowing stairs and rattle open a metal gate at the entrance to the women's spa, as if it were some brothel speakeasy. Rumor has it that the men's spa one floor up features one, ahem, service beyond the offerings at the women's establishment. But this is yet to be proven.

Once through the gate, the front desk, lockers and changing area all reside in one room. That means you hand the cashier your $120 for a two-hour session, and then walk ten feet to the lockers and strip. They give you a robe, which stays on for all of ten more feet—from your locker to the white-tiled room, an immaculate temple filled with tubs of water, flowing showerheads and dripping steam.

There, the tenderizing begins. The first step is the shower. If you don't appear to be washing yourself well enough or fast enough, the ladies may step in and take over, jerking your arms up to get into your armpits and even coming dangerously close to goosing your bare butt with their bare hands. Then they throw you in the steam room for 15 minutes, sometimes pulling you out to douse you with an exhilarating bucket of cold water.

Like some whole fryer chicken, you are dumped onto a plastic cot and begin stage two, the scrub. Armed with scrubbing gloves, the ladies proceed to exfoliate the dead skin, which you'll see cascading off in little clumps as they rinse you with buckets of warm water. A mirror lines the wall in front of you, so you catch glimpses not only of your own bare ass, but on occasion, that of the woman on the neighboring cot. After a stint in the dry sauna, you return to the cot for a ferocious massage. They slather you in oil and then jump on your back, the better to dig deeper and deeper into your muscles, occasionally hitting bone. You emerge glowing and soft as a rose petal and almost light-headed with calm (or trauma, hard to tell which).

Throughout the entire shellacking, no English is spoken. The Yi Pak women just lead you by the arm, make a decisive gesture and say "tuh-tuh-tuh!" Do as they say, and you'll be rewarded.

WEIRD FOR A DAY

(OR MAYBE A WEEK)

Blessing of the Animals

Bring your camels and porcupines to the holy water.

Where: St. John the Divine Cathedral, 1047 Amsterdam Ave., at 110th St.
When: During the Feast of St. Francis in early October, check schedule
Phone: 212-316-7490
Getting there: 1 to Cathedral Pkwy./
110th St.; B,C to 110th St./Cathedral Pkwy.
Fee: Free for standing room, first come, first serve
Website: stjohndivine.org

Whether it's hosting avant-garde artists in controversial performances or filling its outer garden with free-roaming, screaming peacocks, the Cathedral of St. John the Divine in Morningside Heights adds its own distinct seasoning to conventional religious fare. Consider the Feast of St. Francis, when all of God's creatures can find refuge, at least for one day a year, in the world's largest Gothic cathedral.

For several hours, camels, porcupines, monkeys, a golden eagle and reindeer —all of which defecate at will with no shame—march through the cathedral interior in a surprisingly orderly fashion. The most entertaining mischief at a recent Blessing of the Animals involved a llama spitting at onlookers and a sheep chewing the ornamental wreath off the reindeer.

The day's mass features choir singing and African dancers. Seats cost a bundle, but get there early and enjoy standing-room-only for free. Hearing dogs howl in concert with the organ, their voices echoing through the nave, is heartwarming. Afterward, priests offer blessings in the children's garden. People line up with their gerbils, snakes, parrots and other pets. Even heathens can appreciate the priest's sweet blessings, which wish dogs many more sunny days for chasing balls, cats many more naps on warm windowsills, and continued joy to all feathered, furry and four-legged friends.

St. John the Divine stands a fitting venue for any odd event, and this nod to Noah's Ark is no exception. With it's cavernous nave, collapsed buttresses, and unfinished spires, the cathedral is like a disheveled giant that seeks to make itself more inviting. The animals appear at ease here. Dogs don't try to eat the cats, snakes don't gulp the gerbils.

But if you just don't get the charm of fur-covered friends, St. John's holds the Blessing of the Bicycles in April.

Cannoli Eating Contest

Do twenty cannoli taste twenty times better than one?

Where: Northwest corner of Mott and Grand Sts.
When: At the start of the Feast of San Gennaro in September each year
Fee: Free
Getting there: 6, J, M, Z, N, Q, R to Canal St.
Website: sangennaro.org

Certain foods speak of a place. And while eating contests occur all over the U.S. of A., a cannoli eating contest could only happen in Little Italy, where Italian heritage meets the excesses of New York.

A cannolo (singular, fyi), for those extra-terrestrials who might be reading this, is a tube of fried pastry dough filled with mildly sweetened ricotta cheese. The crusty shell crumbles deliciously into the creamy interior with each bite, so slow savoring, rather than hasty pastry popping, is the preferred method of consumption.

New Yorkers enjoy a time-honored tradition of arguing over who makes the best cannoli, parsing the freshness of the pastry, the ratio of crust to ricotta, the nuances of the vanilla, orange, cinnamon or rosewater flavoring. But cannoli-eating contestants leave that kind of talk for the nibblers of the world. On this day, most of the filling runs down chins, beards and arms, and gulps of water turn the crispy crust soggy. There is no savoring here but for the victor.

Major League Eating, the same people who bring you the July 4th Hot Dog Eating Contest (see page 130), kick off the Feast of San Gennaro with this creamy contest each year, and Ferrara Cafe supplies contestants with amply delicious cannoli for devouring. The stage sits on the corner of Mott and Grand with seats available first come, first serve. But you can stand to the side and watch the current contenders—Crazy Legs Conti, Pat from Mounaka, Sean Gordon and Kevin Bass—woof 'em down in profile. The side is also a cherry spot to score leftover cannoli once the action is over. Tim "Eater X" Janus currently holds the record with 26 cannoli eaten.

Cynics will decry any Little Italy establishment as being inferior Italian, but that's irrelevant. Here everyone loves cannoli and they are especially good when free. Grab a couple, walk a few blocks for a cup of cappuccino at Café Palermo. Enjoy it, and tell the naysayers to suck on their sour grapes. Viva faux Italia!

Coney Island Mermaid Parade

The sea coughs up kitsch on the boardwalk.

Where: Coney Island Boardwalk
When: June, check website for schedule
Fee: Free
Website: coneyisland.com

The city's public assembly laws provide great latitude for artistic expression, and nowhere in broad daylight is that latitude more apparent than at the Mermaid Parade.

Every year since 1983, marauding pirates, men with strategically placed swordfish and mermaids in nothing but body paint and a fishtail have marched through the ramshackle streets of Coney Island. The parade ambles along the decaying boardwalk, rusty, protruding nails underfoot, crashing waves to the left, Shoot-the-Freak barker to the right. It sullies the shadow of well-scrubbed KeySpan Park, and then splashes down Surf Avenue retracing its steps towards the shrieks of the rumbling Cyclone. The bouillon

odor of Nathan's, the tinny carnival melodies, hollers from a restless, sweaty crowd all coalesce around an unleashing of inhibitions.

Morality and development, the enduring spoilsports of America, so far threaten the parade in vain. When in 2001 police cited a bare-breasted marcher for indecency, a judge threw out the case, and the woman successfully sued police for $10,000. Rumors flew that the 2007 parade would be its last due to developers moving in, but the mer-march has continued in recent summers, despite Astroland's demise.

The parade traipses on with all but genitalia on display, yet somehow innocence prevails. Strangely enough, ogling tah-tahs isn't what this parade is about. Amidst the mayhem you find a grade-school girl in a parrot costume on six-foot stilts and little mer-girls accompanied by their bathyal fathers rising from the depths. At the parade's climax, King Neptune and Queen Mermaid cut ribbons to open the Atlantic Ocean for the summer season. Everyone along the parade route vows to march in the next year's parade. But then self-consciousness reigns us back in, and we find ourselves once again begging Mardi Gras beads off the lucky, carefree few.

Coney Island Polar Bear Plunge

The annual New Year's nut numbing.

Where: Coney Island Beach
When: New Years Day at 1 p.m., and most Sundays from
October–April at 1 p.m.
Fee: Free
Website: PolarBearClub.org

Many people claim that cold-water swims can cure such ailments as tuberculosis or genital inflammation. Some consider winter swimming a spiritual practice, a disciplined test of will power. Psychic self-regulation they call it. But for most, a dip in an icy ocean seems just plain fucking crazy.

Water temperatures in January average 36 degrees F in New York's waters, not counting the wind chill. These numbers don't dissuade hundreds of New Year's revelers from curing their hangovers with a mad dash for the Atlantic. And, for some, the Polar Bear Plunge might not be the most daring or dumbest thing they've done in the previous 24 hours. But balled-up fists, frantic hopping and wild screeching tell the more sane observers onshore that the anesthetizing breakers have delivered the greatest shock.

Members of the Coney Island Polar Bear Club don't reserve this insanity for one day of the year. They toss themselves into the frigid waters every Sunday at 1 p.m. from October through the end of April. A dedicated crew since 1903, the Polar Bears span every age, ethnicity and fitness level. In recent years, they secured a changing room at the New York Aquarium, which makes the weekly baptism a bit more comfortable. The group organizes the Plunge around various charities, for the Special Olympics in the past and currently for Camp Sunshine, which serves terminally ill children and their families.

Studies have shown that people in colder locales are happier and friendlier than those in lower latitudes. Judging from the camaraderie, the smiles, the unleashing of pure joy, this chilly nostrum at the very least cures a day's worth of mid-winter blues.

The Dance of the Giglio

300 brawny goombahs dancing with a brass band on their shoulders.

Where: Our Lady of Mount Carmel Roman Catholic Church; N. 8th St. and Havemeyer St., in Willamsburg
When: Annually, in mid-July
Getting there: L to Bedford Ave.
Fee: Free
Website: olmcfeast.com

Every July, the hipsters of Williamsburg give way to an outburst of Italian-American pride. The ten-day-long Feast of Our Lady of Mt. Carmel and San Paolino draws tens of thousands of true paisanos from throughout the tri-state area.

The Feast dates back 1,500 years, although Italian immigrants brought the celebration to Williamsburg just over 100 years ago. It honors San Paolino, a fifth-Century philanthropist who gave his freedom in exchange for a boy who had been forced into slavery by the invading Huns. When one of the leaders of the Huns heard the man's story, he returned San Paolino along with all of the captured villagers to their town, where they were greeted with lilies. Each year, in the Italian town of Nola, residents repeated the celebration, and each year, the height and the abundance of lilies grew. Eventually, the Giglio (Italian for "lily") became a four-ton, 85-foot-tall tower festooned with lilies and images of the Virgin Mary and San Paolino. Men hoist the tower and parade it around in a display of penance and machismo.

In Williamsburg, on the two Sundays and on one night midweek, the Dances of the Giglio are held. More than 300 brawny goombahs lift two separate structures, the Giglio, which holds the priest and a 12-piece brass band on the pedestal, and also a wooden ship, weighing upwards of three tons. The participants are broken into a hierarchy of lifters, lieutenants, capos and the capo paranzo, who coordinates the Giglio lift. Generations of men have handed down the honor of performing the Dance of the Giglio.

The capo paranzo shouts "Musica!," and the band strikes up "Funiculi, Funicula." On the Capo's command, the lifters hoist the Giglio and begin the grueling three-hour-long march down Havemeyer and North 8th Streets. Working as a single unit under the direction of the capo, they bounce, sway and cha-cha the deceptively sturdy obelisk. As the weight digs deep into their shoulders, the lifters contemplate their sins, deceased relatives and the merciful Blessed Mother Mary (because in the Roman

Catholic Church, no matter the saint, it all goes back to Mary). With the safety issues and the chaos of the crowd, the capos are burdened with a huge responsibility and are graced with much respect. When they shout "move!," the crowd obeys, parting the streets for the meandering route.

The Dance is a dizzying display of danger, religious devotion and elevated levels of testosterone, mixed with zepole, sausage and peppers and cannoli. Stir it up in a pot, and in the Italian tradition, there's always enough to go around.

Dyker Heights Lights

A Brooklyn neighborhood's plan to trigger an East Coast blackout.

Where: Dyker Heights in Brooklyn, from 80th to 86th Sts., between 10th and 13th Avenues; Best viewing, 83rd and 84th Sts.
When: Thanksgiving until January 6 (the last of the twelve days of Christmas)
Getting there: R to 86th St.
Fee: Free

As roped-off tourists do a slack-jawed shuffle to view Christmas window displays in midtown, a shrieking cry for attention emanates from deep in the heart of Brooklyn. Look southeastward from a Manhattan building top and perhaps you can see the million-watt schlock being cast from Dyker Heights. There, the city's true competition for the most crowd-pleasing holiday spectacle resides.

Littering the yard with plastic candy canes and spotlit Baby Jesuses is a tradition that goes back for generations in Italian-American neighborhoods such as Bensonhurst, Carnarsie and Bay Ridge. But well-to-do Dyker Heights takes the crown for electrified kitsch. As the holiday tourist season approaches, a few Yuletide-inspired Dyker Heights residents invite those in the know to enjoy an independently funded extravaganza of lights. These well-heeled townies seem to be saying, "Keep Manhattan, your storied Rockettes, Rockefeller Tree, ice rink and shoulder-to-shoulder crowds! Give me your fed-up, your 'Claus-traphobic,' your totally over it New Yorkers. I hoist my two-story illuminated nutcracker beside my life-size manger door!"

Brooklynites cherish their well-kept secret, although with 100,000 visitors annually, "secret" may not apply. Bus tours escort the faint-hearted to the far reaches of this nearby outer borough. Traffic jams clog the pinnacle blocks of 83rd and 84th streets between 11th and 13th avenues. The residents of these Victorian and Queen Anne mansions spend tens of thousands on such décor as faux dancing bear topiaries, life-size scenes from Dickens' "A Christmas Carol" and an outsized Santa chummily sitting with his foot crossed over his knee. One house features an international theme, another boasts an army of glowing choir angels. Keep in mind, in

the off-season, a good many of these folks find gate-tending statues of lions, tigers and Grecian ladies the height of good taste.

Some of the expense is surely driven not by the Christmas spirit but by good old-fashioned one-upmanship. Some disgruntled neighbors do wish the log-jammed showcase was gone. But the garish wonderland remains an innocent treat for kids and adults alike in an era when authentic experiences, whatever their origins, are hard to come by. For out-of-towners, this also provides a chance to see the real Brooklyn in all its glory.

Skip on the price-gouging tour buses that charge $100 per couple for something that's free to locals. Take the R to 86th St. and hoof it, or better yet, find a friend with a car and a map. When you're done there, fuel up on cappuccino and dolci at Mona Lisa's Bakery (1476 86th St. at 15th Ave.; monalisabakery.com), and then wander through Bensonhurt and Bay Ridge to chance upon some other illuminated houses. You won't regret the trip, but you may soon look disparagingly at that chintzy chain of tinsel you've been calling a decoration.

Gay Pride Parade

If only because LGBT's really know how to party.

Where: From 5th Ave. and 52nd St. to Christopher and Greenwich Sts.
When: The Sunday nearest June 28th
Fee: Free
Website: nycpride.org

Are men in drag taboo these days? Are butch lesbians on motorcycles shocking? Is a bearded senior citizen flitting around in a petticoat and sequins with a parrot on his head and a dyed-pink poodle in his arms the least bit odd? Who knows? But every year this parade is still a head-shaking romp you don't want to miss.

The best part of New York City's Gay Pride Parade may be watching buttoned-up politicians like Mayor Michael Bloomberg proudly marching alongside all these iconoclasts. And not only do they march, but in 2008 New York's blind, black Governor David Patterson—briefly heralded in the gay community for his state-level advocacy—elicited a riotous cheer from the crowd.

Technically a march, the event commemorates the "hairpin drop heard round the world." On June 28, 1969 at 1 a.m., the NYPD staged a politically motivated raid on the Stonewall Inn, a gay bar in the West Village. An angry crowd of patrons spilled onto Christopher Street. Defiance that started with catcalls escalated to using a parking meter as a battering ram, trapping police in the bar, and then torching it. The police beat those individuals who defied gender stereotypes most blatantly, but over the next five days a mob of one thousand protesters gathered and over-whelmed the riot squad. It was the official start of the LGBT (Lesbian, Gay, Bisexual and Transgender) movement.

A far cry from its anarchic roots, today's parade includes more well-crafted slogans and banners than chants and fists. In fact, even with men in sailor dresses and platform porn pumps, some New Yorkers accuse this event of being too squeaky clean, too mainstream. Yet, as pro-gay-marriage legislation tanks around the country and same-sex partnerships struggle for recognition by America's healthcare providers, those early days don't seem so far behind us. In and among the banners and politicians you'll see the vestiges of those outrageous forebears, the once-persecuted people—in bondage, feathers and false lashes—who bravely embraced the light of day, no longer chased from shadow to shadow.

Greenwich Village Halloween Parade

Funky ghouls and goblins haunt the world's largest Halloween parade.

Where: Route starts at Spring and Canal Sts. to 23rd St.; enter from the south and east
When: Every year, October 31st, 7 p.m.
Fee: Free
Website: Halloween-nyc.com

Every day the New Yorker's inner miscreant aches for chaos while performing our antlike crawl through the subway system, our robotic march to work, our automaton rituals of daily labors. But on October 31st, we cloak ourselves in preternatural armor and unleash our inner demons in the largest Halloween parade in the world. The vast exorcism roils for a full mile up the Avenue of the Americas, with 60,000 costumed marchers, two million onlookers and one million more witnessing the spectacle on TV.

In 1973, puppet-maker Ralph Lee gathered a ragtag group for the first Village ramble, hoping to revive the floundering holiday in the wake of tainted candy scares and surging crime. The parade has since become New Yorkers' gift to themselves. Massive skeleton puppets lead the Village Parade as a symbol of beings that know best what they've lost...and that is life. Behind them, a rollicking raggle-taggle army of the undead performs its duty frightening the crowd.

If you find yourself watching from behind the police barricade, you've made your first mistake. Glue on oozing scars and devil horns (you'll find plenty of costume stores throughout Greenwich Village in the weeks before Halloween), cross the barricade at Spring Street and Sixth Avenue, and watch children's faces morph from thrilled to horrified as they tread the line between nightmare and reality. When you hear the sound of

"Thriller" creeping into the air, stop and stare. Scores of ghouls are about to hobble through the best dance ever choreographed. (Go to Thrillernyc.com to join the dance.)

Procession of Ghouls

The church plays host to, well, the devil and his minions.

Where: Cathedral of St. John the Divine, 1047 Amsterdam Ave., at 110th St.
When: Usually October 30th, check website
Fee: $20, reserve tickets ahead
Website: stjohndivine.org

After Ralph Lee's beloved Village Halloween Parade took on a life of its own, the puppet master of macabre helped start another spooky New York City tradition, the Procession of Ghouls at St. John the Divine. Few if any venues in the entire city can match the looming eeriness of this immense gothic cathedral. The pallor of the limestone, the dark soaring ceiling, and the fang-like arches create the perfect backdrop for this Halloween extravaganza.

In 1990, the Church decided they wanted to celebrate Halloween with classic silent horror flicks set to music from the Aeolian-Skinner Great Organ. They turned to Lee, an artist-in-residence, to create a grand finale to follow the film. Lee gathered his most grotesque hobgoblin puppets to stalk the cavernous nave. Giant skeletons, grotesque pigs, a kind of satanic snapping turtle and dozens of other fiendish wraiths slither through gloomily lit fog, haunting onlookers perched at the edges of their seats. Renowned organist Tim Brumfield provides a suitably scary, improvised soundtrack, adding an aural specter.

According to Lee, some of the more conservative members of the church "look a little askance" at this well-attended event. But at the time of the event's founding, church leaders Paul Moore and James Morton felt that St. John the Divine's mission should resemble that of medieval times, when churches stood at the center of the community and allowed all sorts of peculiar events to take place. "If the Church is going to be threatened by some papier mache masks, then the Church has some problems," says Lee.

Not this church, baby.

Holi Festival (or Phagwah)

Hindus jump-start spring with a smear-fest of color.

Where: Phil "Scooter" Rizzuto Park, bordered by 95th Ave., 127th St., Atlantic Ave., and 125 St., Brooklyn
When: Late February or early March, check website
Getting there: E to Roosevelt Ave./Jackson Heights, and then Q24 bus to Atlantic Ave./124th St.
Fee: Free
Website: aryaspiritualcenter.com

On a Sunday in late winter the trees in Richmond Hill may be bare, but the landscape takes on the colors of a psychedelic spring: neon pink, electric blue and marigold-yellow. The annual Hindu Holi Festival has arrived.

Celebrating both the triumph of good over evil and the arrival of spring, Holi came to Richmond Hill not from India but from Guyana, Trinidad and Tobago. During the 1800s, British Colonials sent many Hindus to work the sugar cane plantations in the Caribbean. They brought Holi with them as a beloved holiday, but it became known as Phagwah. In 1990, thousands of Indo-Caribbean immigrants, instigated by the Arya Spiritual Center, rekindled this celebration again in Richmond Hill.

It begins in late February or early March with a parade of Desi societies, marching bands, and mandir, or temple, communities, which culminates in Phil Rizzuto Park. Thousands of Indians, from kids to grannies, joyfully smear colored powder on each other's heads in a ritual known as playing Holi or Phagwah. With children wielding Supersoakers full of liquid dye, clothes get blasted, too, for love of the event.

In recent years, because the activities were staining the streets, playing Holi has been restricted to Rizzuto Park. But revelers find opportunity to make mischief, as puffs of powder rise up over the parade and cheeks turn blue in the streets before the police have time to signal the all clear. By the end of the day, the brown winter grass has turned pink and masses of people cheerfully skip away with their faces, their hands and their clothes dyed bright yellow, red and purple.

On those gray days—as New Yorkers long for warm weather to "get here already"—the Holi celebrants seem to have conjured the heat of India and the islands from the cold pavement. The incongruous presence of hyper-rich colors and equally dazzling smiles thaws the winter blues.

Passing Peculiarity

THE STORY OF CHICKEN SOUP SCULPTURE

WHERE: 527 WEST 110TH ST. NEAR AMSTERDAM AVE.

There's no shortage of grinning gargoyles, dragons curled around drainpipes, and other grotesque architectural ornaments lurking above our heads, hanging from lintels, keeping an eye on the city streets below. But on the Upper West Side, a quartet inexplicably makes chicken soup. At the double-winged Brittania apartment building built in 1909, the potage relishing gargoyles hover only 10 feet above the street, so the details are easy to see. One leering figure holds the recipe book, the next samples the broth with his finger from a bowl, the third holds a chicken on a tray, and the fourth laps up soup with delight.

125

Only in New York Stories 4

We witnessed two off-duty cops interrupt a mugging and then shoot at the muggers as they ran off. Both were caught, one more quickly than the other. The perp had run into Farrell's, the notorious cop and fireman bar made famous in Pete Hamill's book 'A Drinking Life.'

— CJ

One morning I was walking my dog, Teddy, to the off-leash area in Prospect Park. Upon entering the Peninsula, nailed at eye level to about twenty trees were fresh goat tongues. Some of the dogs were leaping up and tearing pieces of the tongues from the trees. My guess was the Santería had performed another ritual. This was far more dramatic than the occasionally found offering of chicken parts and herbs placed at the base of a tree.

— ANGELO IZZI

I was driving with my family up Bleecker Street in the 80s and at an intersection a vagrant approached our car. Being suburban, my mom immediately started hitting the buttons, yelling, "Lock the doors! Lock the doors!" When the vagrant crossed our path, we realized it was Grandpa Munster!

— JULIE TENINBAUM

We had this sheltered friend from the South visiting us. We went to a free concert in the park where we immediately encountered a bum lying on a rock—masturbating. Next we witnessed a concert-goer openly peeing on a tree. And finally we returned to Central Park South, where there was a carriage horse with a full erection. Apparently it was Penis Day in Central Park. We spouted the standard "It's not usually like this!"

— SUSAN BOGLE

It was a morning in 1998. A crowded southbound #6 train pulled into 88th Street, but I noticed an almost empty car. As soon as I stepped in I saw a gigantic swishing puddle of human blood on the floor. I freaked out and did a little monkey dance to avoid it as a few seated passengers started giggling. When the doors closed, they all went back to their reading. When we pulled into the next station, everyone on the car dropped their reading again to watch the reaction of people entering. The show continued until 42nd Street when a cop gets on and orders the car cleared. Someone griped, "Ah, just get a mop."

— JOHN GILMORE

Improv Everywhere

Staged spontaneity and acts of mischief by guerilla pranksters.

Where: Anywhere and Everywhere
When: Join the mailing list online to get word of the next "mission"
Fee: Free
Website: ImprovEverywhere.com

Call Improv Everywhere the democratization of theater. Call it an annoying hipster trend. Just don't call it a flashmob, because founder Charlie Todd hates that. And, credit where credit's due, this group's pranks require more thoughtfulness and result in more smiles than that other lemming trend.

Charlie Todd conceived of Improv Everywhere way back in 2001, when he and his friends punked a whole bar into believing that he was musician Ben Folds. His success led him to a life as a stuntman, so to speak. Since then, Todd has broadened his audience and widened his stage. One of the most memorable acts of mischief was Frozen Grand Central, where more than 200 "agents," as the participants are called, froze in time on the main concourse for five full minutes. The effect was striking, as people's brains struggled to reconcile the scene (find it on YouTube).

New Yorkers, those kings of comedy, have willingly played along with many tricks, as when entire sections at Yankee stadium joined in to scream for a seemingly lost guy named Rob, whose friends (planted agents) just couldn't seem to get his attention. Or when passersby stopped to encourage a suicide jumper, teetering on a ledge four feet above the sidewalk, by chanting "Hit the X! Hit the X!"—the mark on the tiny trampoline a "fireman" had placed below the jumper. The group stages pant-less subway rides every January. The event has grown to 1,200 agents in New York and more than 1,000 agents in twenty cities around the world. They also recruit people for mp3 experiments, where scores of people download an mp3, gather in one place and hit play at a set time. A nouveau game of Simon Says ensues.

With more than 85 outrageous scenes to their name, and countless people having witnessed Charlie's staged surreal events, you have to wonder if Improv Everywhere runs the risk of forever killing the spontaneity and serendipity of New York. Will people ever again trust our city's naturally occurring Dadaistic moments? For now, the merry pranksters deliver on the stated goal, "to create scenes of chaos and joy." So, should you find yourself at a "mission," just lose the cynicism and delight in the ride.

The Manhattan Island Marathon Swim

Floating detritus is good for us.

Where: Circumnavigates Manhattan Island, counterclockwise
South Cove to South Cove
When: Begins around 7:30 a.m., one summer Saturday
(check website for date)
Fee: Free to watch
Website: NYCSwim.com

Most people who throw themselves into the Hudson, Harlem and East Rivers are doing so to kill themselves. So what of the Manhattan Island Marathon swimmers? Every year, 25 ultra athletes jump into these challenging waterways to circumnavigate Manhattan Island, from Battery Park City, up the East River, through the vicious, brown Harlem River, and back down the Hudson. They brave ferry wakes, 60-degree waters, waste oil and hypodermic needles for no greater prize than a standard trophy. One could argue that the only difference between these swimmers and the bridge jumpers is that the swimmers prefer to kill themselves slowly.

In 1926, R.W. Dowling, an 18-year-old athlete, made the first successful swim around Manhattan, with many more attempts occurring over the following decades. Drury Gallagher and Tom Hetzel made the first annual swim in 1982, at the height of river filthiness. At that time, corrupt companies routinely dumped their waste into the waters surrounding Manhattan...and mobsters, their hits. Since then, and maybe in small part due to the annual swim, the government has cleaned the waters dramatically; they may be cleaner now than they were 100 years ago. The fish are coming back, and a commission is determining whether and how beaches may soon be opened on the Hudson. Still, it takes a big set of cojones (or perhaps, a shrunken tiny set) to stand at that water's edge and obey the starter's call to jump in.

Extreme athletes count the Manhattan Island Marathon Swim as the third jewel in the triple crown of long-distance swimming, which includes the Catalina and English Channels. At 28.5 miles, the swim stretches six miles longer than the English Channel and equals the effort of three consecutive marathon runs. Entry fees cost more than $1,000 to cover the efforts of race organizers to coordinate the swim, accounting for currents, ferries and cruise ship schedules. It runs counterclockwise around the island to follow the incoming and then outgoing tides and takes anywhere from seven to ten hours. Only 25 solo swimmers and 18 relay groups are allowed and slots fill up within two hours of opening registration.

To watch these outrageous and gutsy swimmers, head to South Cove and Battery Park for the 7:30 a.m. start, the Upper East Side at about 9:00 a.m., anywhere along the Harlem River throughout the mid-morning, then back to the World Financial Center at around 2:00 p.m. The best views are at water level, where those bobbing orange-capped heads look so tiny floating in front of the city's towering edifices.

Nathan's Famous Hot Dog Eating Contest

Gorge and heave!

Where: Nathan's Famous flagship store in Coney Island
When: Noon, every July 4th
Getting there: D, F, Q to Stillwell Ave.
Fee: Free
Website: Nathansfamous.com

Competitive eating falls precisely at the intersection of deadly sin and grueling sport. You watch as eagerly as any fan, rooting your favorite chomper to victory while cringing throughout and praying that no one dies before your very eyes.

The pinnacle of gustatory spectacles is Nathan's Famous Hot Dog Eating Contest, held every July 4th since 1916. There is no denying the sporting aspect of this 10-minute battle among 20 masterful masticators. Witness the veins straining out of reigning champ Joey Chestnut's forehead, the skill in Takeru Kobayashi's precise snatching and jamming of wieners and buns.

Officials from Major-League Eating, the contest's promoter, closely monitor every quarter, half, and whole dog to go down (If you're wondering, vomiting is a disqualification.) Sportswriters can chew on the rivalry between aging former champ Kobayashi and the youthful Chestnut, on the intrigue hovering around relative newcomer Pat Bertoletti (can he upset these veterans?), and on the long shot Sonya "the Black Widow" Thomas, who holds 22 titles but cannot snag the Mustard Yellow Belt.

This is the place to be at noon on the anniversary of our nation's birth, standing in the broiling heat among an international throng of 35,000, listening to the hypnotizing play-by-play commentary of emcee (and promoter) George Shea. At the final bell, these kosher gladiators stand hunched and panting over strewn beef and a roaring crowd. They have sacrificed and inspired. And the masses tip their footlongs to them.

Tugboat Races

The bulldogs of the harbor going for gold in the brackish Hudson.

Where: Hudson River Park, Pier 83
When: Around September (check website)
Getting there: 1, 3, A, C, E to 42nd St., walk west to Hudson River
Website: workingharbor.com

Tugboats, with their smiling hulls and their wheelhouses pushed up on the bow, are the lovable bulldogs of the harbor. They even "toot," for crying out loud. While tugs can be spotted scuttling about the harbor at any time,

tug companies strut their engines once a year at the Annual Great North River Tugboat Races and Competition.

At the end of Pier 83 at Hudson River Park (43rd Street), the Intrepid looms like a retired patriarch in its slip just to the north. Elderly men lean over the railing, sizing up the working and historic tugs circling about the Hudson (formerly known as the North River). Young families let their youngest wriggle through the small crowd for a good view. A spectator boat launches from Pier 83 and follows the line of tugs from the west. They parade up to the 79th St. Boat Basin, where they line up for the start. The sky is bright September blue, the air crisp and the water calm. But not for long.

Tugboats pilot gigantic ships into port and nudge heavily laden barges around the harbor. Their engines boast up to 3,200 horsepower, and when a row of thirteen tugs comes barreling down the river at 12 knots, no small craft wants to be nearby. Yet, for some unknown reason, a small sloop bobbled onto the racecourse during the 2009 event. The wakes tossed it about like a toy, as spectators watched in horror. Two clueless kayakers also sat at the finish line waiting for the tugs, while emcee Capt. John Doswell, of the Working Harbor Committee, screamed over the P.A. for them to move to safety. Miraculously, in both cases, no one was hurt. The unpredictable nature of this busy waterway event gives the entire proceedings a rollicking charm.

Tug crews form families, if not by blood than by the brackish waters of the harbor. These bonds are on display as the crews compete not only in the race, which lasts all of six minutes, but also in nose-to-nose pushing contests and line-toss competitions, in which tugs pull up to the pier and muscled Popeyes heave four-inch-thick lines onto a bollard. One year when they used barges for the line toss, a tug took too aggressive an approach and crashed into the barge it was assigned to. Half the spectators fell off the barge's other side into the water (fortunately, no one was hurt). They now tie up to the pier and use massive camel fenders to protect both city property and onlookers.

After the water competitions, the crews come on land for a spinach-eating contest and a tattoo judging. In 2009, Captain Curt, a man with an expanse of flesh canvas, took top honors for his full-back image of a sinking ship, titled "The Last Watch." Another acknowledgement went to the *Lieutenant Murphy*, which placed last in the tug race, but received the Little Toot award for arriving first at the scene of the Miracle on the Hudson (Captain Sully's amazing January 2009 river landing).

The tug crews, everyday heroes, mostly keep to themselves as awards are handed out at the end of the day. These gruff, weathered men and women work the invisible corners of the harbor, passing each other in the night, speaking through airwaves and air horns, seeking no greater glory than the next haul. But once a year, they go balls out, because, well, everybody needs to let off a little steam sometimes (toot, toot!)

THE ODDER SIDE OF MIDNIGHT

WHETHER YOU'RE SEARCHING OUT WEIRD NEW YORK, OLD NEW YORK, DIRTY NEW YORK, OR AVANT-GARDE NEW YORK, THE PLACES HERE KEEP THE CITY'S HEART RATE UP AFTER DARK. MANY OF THESE ESTABLISHMENTS SURVIVED RENT HIKES, THE RECESSION AND THE REPRESSIVE TACTICS OF THE GIULIANI ERA. SOME HAVE HELD OFF THE CREEP OF YUPPIEDOM, WHILE OTHERS MANAGE TO HOST HIPSTERS AND STILL GIVE YOU A GOOD ENOUGH TIME TO FORGIVE THEM FOR IT.

Bowery Poetry Club

Where: 308 Bowery, near Bleecker St.
Phone: 212-614-0505
Getting there: 6 to Bleecker St.; F to Second Ave.
Website: bowerypoetry.com

Although it's been open only since 2002, the Bowery Poetry Club harnesses the history of its namesake thoroughfare. A venue for spoken word, skewed comedy, burlesque, performance art and poetry slams, BPC continues to hold it down for the punk rock, DIY artist's scene. Future freaks of America can get their art on at Bowery Kids on Sundays. Drag King Murray Hill hosts Monday Night Bingo, an ever-popular event (get there early for a seat).

Cinema Kings Highway

Where: 711 Kings Hwy, Gravesend, Brooklyn
Phone: 718-339-1800
Note: Mostly bi/gay male crowd

It's always after-dark at Cinema Kings Highway. It's also pungent and seedy, and don't even try to identify that rustling going on behind you. Classic movies play on one screen, porn on the other two—old-school porn with big bushes and hairy men. There are also booths for private viewing (yech ... not that there's anything wrong with that). Some places in New York are here to stay. Even the icky ones.

Dances of Vice

When: Check website for upcoming events
Website: dancesofvice.com

Break out your brass goggles. Dances of Vice are overwrought erotic parties drenched in steampunk aesthetic, i.e. punk attitude suited up Victorian-style. Only here, attendants come dressed in every sort of sexy period getup and generally purse their lips and look fabulous. Exotic performers strip and belly dance and play ragtime, classical baroque or otherwise nostalgic tunes. Events generally happen monthly at rotating venues. If you've been to an SCA event (Society for Creative Anachronism), well, you'll know what to expect.

Farrell's Bar

Where: 215 Prospect Park West, between 16th St. and Windsor Pl., Brooklyn
Phone: 718-788-8779
Fee: Cash only

Men go to Farrell's (immortalized in Pete Hammill's *A Drinking Life*) to drink cold Bud in styrofoam cups and watch the game and not get bothered by women or yuppies or the changing cultural landscape of America. They keep the lights bright and the music off so as not to attract the wrong kind of drinker. If you want to steep yourself in this red-blooded scene, don't make an ass of yourself. The barkeep or the patrons—many of whom are cops and firemen and union guys with jobs tougher than yours—will throw you bodily out of the joint. Order the Farrellizer, the 40-oz. cup of Bud. Poured out of the coldest taps in the city, it never tasted so good.

Goodbye Blue Monday

Where: 1087 Broadway, between Dodworth and Lawton Sts., Bushwick, Brooklyn
Phone: 718-453-6343
Getting there: J to Kosciusko St.; J, M, Z to Myrtle Ave.
Website: goodbye-blue-monday.com

This indoor junkyard presents some of the most out-there artists and musicians in the city. Open every day from 11 a.m. on, the antique shop/coffee bar/performance space has been hiding way the hell out in Bushwick for the past decade. Their backyard theater stays open year-round thanks to a good heater, and many nights there is entertainment both indoors and out. Check out the Bushwick Book Club, a beloved night where musicians are invited to compose songs inspired by particular books.

Galapagos Art Space

Where: 16 Main St., between Plymouth St. and Water St., Brooklyn
Phone: 718-222-8500
Getting there: F to York St.; A, C to High St.
Website: galapagosartspace.com

Galapagos Art Space, the sexy librarian of nightspots, is forward thinking in all aspects, being housed in a LEEDS-certified building in the heart of DUMBO. Monday through Friday, you'll find music, think & drink events, experimental theater and dance. Every Saturday at 10:30 p.m., the pasties peek out for the Floating Kabarette, a sexy variety show featuring burlesque and aerial performances. Just be careful, if you're tippling, not to topple into the shallow ponds of water that dot the interior (yes, there are ponds of water used in the design scheme).

House of Yes

Where: 342 Maujer St., near Morgan Ave., Ridgewood, Brooklyn
When: Check website for upcoming shows.
Getting there: L to Grand St.
Website: houseofyes.org

Want to know where some strong-willed, do for ya'self, freaky-deaky art is happening? Head to the House of Yes, where the resident company puts on highly skilled aerial performances (it's home to Lady Circus), multimedia installations and experimental musical theater in a huge space. They also offer sewing and craft instruction, aerial skills and movement classes, as well as an occasional class for men titled "This Ain't Your High School Sex Ed Class," where men learn that they need to go downtown more often than they think.

KGB Bar/Kraine Theater/ The Red Room

Where: 85 E. 4th St., between Second Ave. and the Bowery
When: Check website for upcoming shows.
Getting there: F, V to 2nd Ave-Houston St.; 6 to Bleecker St-Lafayette
Phone: 212-505-3360
Website: kgbbar.com; nyneofuturists.org

Denis Woychuck founded the Kraine Theater in 1984 in the former home of the Ukrainian Working Men's Club. The KGB Bar and The Red Room followed. The KGB Bar readings are fine, but for a truly heady cultural experience, catch Too Much Light Makes the Baby Go Blind on Friday and Saturday nights. This is when the New York Neo-Futurists make a concerted attempt to perform 30 plays in 60 minutes. No other theater troupe in the city works this hard.

Lips

Where: 2 Bank St., at Greenwich Ave.
Phone: 212-675-7710
Getting there: 1, 2, 3 to 14th St.
Website: lipsnyc.com
Notes: Reservations required. Check website to see their rules about food/drink minimums and an entertainment surcharge.

The go-to drag joint for bachelorette parties and other events that call for giddy squealing, Lips gives all its guests the queen's treatment. The cross-dressing entertainers are also your servers, so the fun gets going from the moment you sit down. Lips offers a full night of entertainment Tuesdays through Saturdays, and hits late risers with a Sunday Gospel Brunch.

Lucky Cheng's

Where: 24 First Ave., between 1st and 2nd Sts.
Phone: 212-995-5500
Getting there: F, V to Second Ave.
Fee: Reservations required for dinner. $32 per person includes a
3-course pan-Asian meal and show
Website: planetluckychengs.com

Another drag queen dinner theater, much like Lips, but maybe a little cattier.

Nuyorican Poets Cafe

Where: 236 E 3rd St., between Ave. B and Ave. C
Phone: 212-505-8183
Getting there: F to Second Ave.
Website: nuyorican.org

You might catch a bad performance here, but Nuyorican is always packed for good reason—at least one artist will make your trip to Alphabet City worth the trek. Founded in 1973, Nuyorican has maintained its grassroots dedication to artists, and as such, the vibe in the place is warm and supportive. Thursdays, you'll find Latin Jazz, while Fridays get super packed for the poetry slam. Hang in there through some melodramatics—someone will eventually hit gold. Check the schedule for hip-hop, comedy, theatre and multimedia performances.

Public Assembly

Where: 70 North 6th St., between Wythe and Kent Sts.,
Williamsburg, Brooklyn
When: Check website for upcoming shows
Phone: 718-384-4586
Getting there: L to Bedford Ave.
Website: publicassemblynyc.com

The former home of Galapagos Art Space now houses Public Assembly. Check out some lowbrow titillation at Monday Night Burlesque (that's every Monday night) and the much-loved monthly Bunker Parties, where you get some of the city's best electronic dance music in a communist-like industrial setting. Public Assembly also hosts bands, open mikes, films, karaoke and comedy.

Pussycat Lounge and Shogun Room

Where: 96 Greenwich St., between Carlisle and Rector Sts.
When: Check website for upcoming shows
Phone: 212-349-4800
Website: pussycatloungenyc.com

This monument to New York sleaze faced extinction when developers tried to tear it down to put up a hotel. Fortunately, due to a good fight from the owner (whom the The New York *Times* called "New York's first and only strip-club-owning preservationist"), the landmark flesh palace was saved. The split-personality venue offers bands, DJs and cabaret performances upstairs. Downstairs, you'll find bored-looking strippers gyrating behind the bar. Patrons can get lap dances in a discreet room to the side. The regulars, all of a sort, are worth a gander as well.

An aside: Cordato's Bodega (94 Greenwich St.) right next door seems like a normal deli in the front, but there's a bar through an unmarked door in the back. The waitresses used to offer $10 lap dances, but the city reined it in. Now, very scantily clad Latina ladies back the bar.

Slipper Room

Where: 167 Orchard St. at Stanton St.
When: Check website for upcoming shows
Phone: 212-253-7246
Getting there: F to Second Ave.; J, M, Z, F to Essex St.–Delancey
Website: slipperroom.com

The bawdy, tawdry Slipper Room serves up neo-burlesque six days a week, but they give libidos a break every Tuesday for some stand-up comedy. The shows start at ten and run all night long. It's just $5 to get in, with no drink minimum and no reservations required. Mr. Choade's Upstairs/Downstairs, their Saturday party, has been running continuously since 1999 and is the longest running burlesque show in New York.

Subway Inn

Where: 143 E. 60th St., near Lexington Ave.
Getting there: 4, 5, 6 to 59th St.; N, R, W to Fifth Ave. and 59th St.
Phone: 212-223-8929
Website: Ha!

Sometimes, a darkened room with sticky tables, crusty regulars and a signature odor feels like the best place in the world to have a drink. Noted both for being laidback and unpredictable, Subway Inn hosts one of the oddest mixes of patrons in all of New York City. Blue- and white-collar, young and old, upstanding and miscreant, anyone can find a place at the bar, while troublemakers might catch a boot out the door. Dating back to the '30s, its placement right across from Bloomies shows that our city can still maintain the crux of its absurdist personality.

Sunny's in Red Hook

Where: 253 Conover St., near Reed St., Brooklyn
When: Open Wednesday, Friday and Saturday 8 p.m–4 a.m.; cash only
Getting there: B61 bus to Van Brunt and Beard Sts. from A, C, F to Jay St.; B77 Bus to Van Brunt St. and Van Dyke St. from F, G at Smith and 9th Sts.
Phone: 718-625-8211
Website: sunnysredhook.com

Open in 1890 by the current owner's great-great-grandfather, Sunny's started out as a longshoremen's bar. Today, it's still a place where regular folks come to drink beer, not sip cosmos. It retains its funky, old-timey charm, in part because it's so damn hard to get to, way off the subway line, down by the water and close to by Bob Diamond's abandoned streetcar tracks (see Abandoned Subway Tunnel page 14). Regularly voted best dive bar, Sunny's also hosts some fine musicianship at their bluegrass jamborees.

Upright Citizen's Brigade Theater

Where: 307 W. 26th St., between 8th and 9th Aves.
When: Check website for upcoming shows
Phone: 212-366-9176
Getting there: C, E to 23rd St.
Website: ucbtheater.com

Improvisers create comedy out of thin air, like a bunch of stand-up MacGyvers. Which also means that at UCB, the performers can easily hit the wrong comedy triggers at any moment and bomb big time. It happens. In the theater's tight basement space (with the duct-taped seats), UCB's experimental artists go balls out testing new material nightly and it can be amazingly funny or marginal. But the cheap $10 ticket price kind of assures that you don't care. There's an excellent chance of stumbling upon a sketch comedian you recognize from the telly, too. The graduates of the UCB Theater School also write for many of your favorite shows, like SNL (the good years and the bad) and The Office. Think you could do what they do? Then take a class. You'll get to perform onstage in front of a New York audience at the end of your semester. After that, you'll forever think twice about heckling.

Passing Peculiarity

UNION SQUARE METRONOME

WHERE: SOUTH END OF UNION SQUARE

Everyone wonders what the hell that crazy counter is all about. So pay attention: the 15 numbers of the digital clock display how much time has passed in the day and how much time remains. You read time passed from left to right and time remaining in the opposite direction. Got that? Just to be sure, here's what the explanation from the Union Square website says: "… if the clock reads 070437000235616, it means that it is 7:04 A.M. and that there are 16 hours, 56 minutes and 23 seconds remaining until midnight." The three numbers in between are hundredths of a second, and they're just a blur. The rest of it, with the steam and whatnot, is just some artsy-fartsy crap.

141

BIZARRE BYGONES

Gone but not forgotten, these venerable institutions, colorful characters, and even chickens, once helped define a New York State of mind.

mato Opera

Where: 319 Bowery at Bleecker St.
b. 1948; closed 2009

Orchestra seats at the Met go for up to $300. The cheapest seats, at $20, are situated more than five stories above the stage because, apparently, us poor people suck. But once upon a time, sucky poor people who loved the opera had a place to go—the Amato Opera. There, a front row seat at a lovingly staged production cost, at most, $35.

Tony Amato, along with his wife Sally, started the Amato Opera in 1948, performing the classics in small venues around the city and passing a hat at the end of the show. At one point, both Amatos pursued larger operatic ambitions, but when that endeavor proved fruitless, they settled for a smaller dream in a cozier theater. In 1962, the Amatos opened their own opera house, considered the world's smallest, on the Bowery. Tickets were $4. This stretch of New York was skid row at the time, so each morning Tony politely swept the bums and their refuse off of his front sidewalk to ready his venue for the night's performance.

For decades, Amato staged Verdi and Wagner just a few doors from the venerable punk club, CBGB's. Tony scurried about the house working the sound, moving props, directing the cast and conducting the bare bones orchestra, while Sally sewed costumes, fed cast and crew Italian food and did the books. Dedicated to developing young talent, Tony changed the cast every night to allow more singers to perform. He scheduled just one rehearsal for each show and paid his principals $10. More than two dozen of Amato's protégées ultimately went on to the Met and the City operas.

Many reviewers considered his staging and his conducting to be genius. During particularly big operas, the performers piled onto the stage like it was a clown car, but Tony's stage direction arranged them neatly and moved them about seamlessly—except on occasion. With so little rehearsal and an uneven cast, productions would sometimes go awry. Tony often would sing along, sometimes a necessity when a weak voice couldn't carry or when performers lost their way. When a stage curtain broke, the show temporarily halted while Tony fixed the problem. But both the intimacy and onstage quirkiness charmed the audience; the theater's flaws became part of its beauty.

Sally passed away in 2000, but Tony kept the opera going until May of 2009, when he sold the locally famous, narrow white building. Originally purchased for $22,000, it fetched $3.7 million, proceeds Amato now uses to fund scholarships for singers, stage directors and young opera conductors.

roken Angel

Where: 4/6 Downing St., Brooklyn
Getting there: G to Classon Ave.
b. 1979; d. 2007
Note: Remnants of the Broken Angel architecture remain on the building's façade.

In the wake of the recession, New York City has been littered with unfinished buildings facing orders to cease construction for code violations and/or lack of funds. For most of these "luxury" blights, there's no love lost. But one peculiar structure captured the city's heart and imagination. The Broken Angel House rose like a phoenix above Clinton Hill, jutting hither and thither, pillar to post, following the capricious architectural whims of owner Arthur Wood.

Wood bought the former Brooklyn Trolley headquarters in 1979, feeling that its burned-out roof and crumbling walls held potential. He moved in with his wife and two children, and rather than spend his money on improvements to make his home more inhabitable—for instance, there was no reliable heat source—Wood attempted to create a masterpiece in timber and glass.

Above the red door, which read "Broken Angel," Wood constructed an inverted stained glass steeple that protruded from the façade. On top of the original rooftop, he built an asymmetrical structure that was wider on top than bottom and rose a precarious 40 feet into the air. The building provided a backdrop for

Dave Chappell's Block Party and also was the subject of a 1991 documentary. Broken Angel captured the anarchic, artistic, unbalanced and stubborn will of the city, and few chose to argue with its aesthetic merits.

However, when fire struck in 2007, firefighters were forced to take position outside the building, because the lack of an interior stairwell and gaping holes in the floor made it unsafe to enter. In the aftermath, the Buildings Department found a bevy of code violations. Wood claimed he had complete plans, supervised by an architect and in line with code. But the Buildings Department saw a structure that no permit would have allowed.

A developer subsequently collaborated with Wood to bring the building up to code and transform it into a multiuse dwelling. It would house condos, an art school and a museum, as well as Wood and his wife. Development began, but the entire top structure had to be removed. Eventually, with the project under-capitalized, foreclosure struck. Wood was issued an order to vacate, and he and his wife, who was then suffering from cancer, were forced to move out. The developer put the house up for sale in January 2009 for $4 million. At printing, the fate of the building, and of the Woods, was unknown.

The Dancing and Tic-Tac-Toe Playing Chickens

Where: 8 Mott St.
b. 1960s; d. 1998

No chicken in New York has ever been more famous than the World Famous Dancing and Tic-Tac-Toe Chickens at the Chinatown Fair store. For four decades, a series of birds strutted their stuff and took on all comers in a clash of wits and strategy.

Drop 75 cents in the slot, and the dancing chicken, playing second fiddle in the back of the arcade, would step out onto her miniature stage and flap her wings and shuffle her feet in a feathered soft-shoe. While many believed the metal stage was electrified, it was simply a wobbly tray that caused the bird to teeter about trying to regain her balance.

The Tic-Tac-Toe Chicken performed beneath a sign that asked: "Bird Brain, Can you beat this bird?" For a couple quarters, the bird stepped out to meet your tic-tac challenge, but she always got first move. And she always won. Of course, the game was rigged and the hen simply pecked around—but never mind that. When do you get to play a game against a feathered beast?

Animal rights activists shrilly tried to shut the game down for years. In 1998, a man named Patrick Kwan and an elderly woman finally convinced the owner of the Chinatown Fair to relinquish the one remaining chicken. Lillie, as she was called, lived out her remaining days on a farm in Massachusetts. The arcade owner promised not to bring the act back, but you can head down to the Tropicana in Atlantic City, where the Tic-Tac-Toe chickens have re-emerged. There, a tic-tac-toe win pays off at ten grand, quite a bit better than the Chinatown Fair's measly bag of fortune cookies.

The Gay Club Scene

Where: Mostly in Greenwich Village
b. late 1800s; wounded in battle in the 1980s

New York's relatively permissive attitude toward the gay scene has drawn queer lifestylers from around the world for more than a century. Our gay clubs have run the gamut from a literary bar like the San Remo, which opened in 1925 and catered to the likes of John Cage and Jack Kerouac, to the hardcore Mineshaft, whose fliers advertised evenings of "Golden Showers Activities."

The Slide, which opened around 1890 at 157 Bleecker Street, was the first known drag club. While most other gay clubs cultivated anonymity, the Slide earned the nickname "the wickedest place in New York" for being the most debauched. Recognizing an opportunity in illicit behavior, organized crime muscled in to run many of the city's gay clubs, including the San Remo. The mafia also laid claim to drag clubs like Club 181 at 181 2nd Avenue, whose doors were open from the mid-30s to 1953, and Club 82 at 82 E. 4th Street, open from 1953 (now a porno theater).

Then there were the baths, including the notorious Everard Baths at 28 West 28th Street. Open from 1888 to 1985, the baths attracted a gay celebrity clientele that included Gore Vidal, Rudolph Nureyev and Truman Capote. A tragic fire killed nine men at the baths in 1977. Health authorities closed Everard for good in 1985, during the AIDS crisis.

The Stonewall Inn, also run by the mob, marked the site of the 1969 riots and the start of the gay rights movement. In the post-Stonewall era, the Mineshaft, the Crisco Disco and the Anvil took depravity to new lows. The Anvil featured a downstairs porno theater with sawdust covering the floor. At the Crisco Disco, one could find piles of cocaine and open sex. But the Mineshaft trumped all, with its S&M dungeon, its room off the dance floor outfitted with "glory holes," and its large tub available for the aforementioned golden-shower "watersports." Reaction to the AIDS crisis also shut this venue down in 1985. Today, a Thai restaurant stands in its place at 835 Washington Street. If the patrons only knew what once went on where the kitchen now stands.

Joe Ades, The Carrot Peeler Man

b. December 18, 1933; d. February 1, 2009

His voice drifted up and over the crowd and reached you before you ever saw him. "You've never used a peeler so sharp or comfortable in your life," Joe Ades would call out during his vegetable-peeler pitch. The passersby would stop, drawn to this elderly dapper figure, who was said to wear thousand-dollar suits, eat at the finest restaurants, and sip champagne as his drink of choice. Yet, six days a week, he squatted on a campstool in green markets or on street corners slicing carrots and potatoes for a living (Ades was married to a Park Avenue woman, and lived comfortably in her uptown apartment, so his survival did not depend on his peeler patter).

Ades delivered his four-minute spiel the same way every time, using classic huckster tactics with his refined sales pitch. First, he asked that people move closer. "It's just a common courtesy. I won't ask you for money. I just don't want to have to yell," he'd say. Next, he used the peeler to make flower shaped carrot slices—"This'll get the kiddies to eat their vegetables!" Then he peeled a potato, cut eyes out of it, sliced French fries and used it as a mandolin to slice potato chips. By now he'd have drawn a crowd and transfixed them all. With a flourish, he reached into his pocket and pulled out a wad of bills. (Nothing spurs spending like the sight of cold hard cash.) Now came the pitch: "$5 for one, five for $20." Instantly, wallets opened, and fives and twenties would fly between Ades and his customers. Within 30 seconds, he could sell $100 worth of peelers, the continuous melody of the pitch never ceasing for a moment.

Born in Manchester, England, Ades learned his trade as a teenager from the grafters who sold goods amid the rubble of World War II. Although he sold many products during his lifetime, the peeler—"Made in Switzerland, stainless steel, it'll never rust!"—made him famous over the last 15 years of his life. *The Daily News, Vanity Fair* and even the Today Show documented his storied rise from street pitchman to Park Avenue bon vivant. Yet, he still had to dodge the police as he sold his goods without a permit at the Union Square Greenmarket.

While his tactics may have skirted the law, Ades didn't push faulty wares. "You don't buy these because they're cheap. You buy them because they're good and they work," he asserted. Thousands of New Yorkers heeded his advice. In the days after his death, message boards filled with people relating their memories of this iconic oddball, a mainstay of New York street life who sold the best peeler ever.

*T*ower of Toys

Where: Sixth St. and Avenue B Community Garden
b. Early 1980s; d. May 19, 2008

The Junk Tower or Tower of Toys and its creator, Eddie Boros, loomed over the community garden at Avenue B and 6th Street for more than two decades. While many likened it to the masterly and sturdy Watts Towers in L.A., the Junk Tower always looked one corroded nail away from disaster. Wooden planks climbed willy-nilly 65 feet into the neighborhood's stout skyline. Stuffed animals decayed as they hung by their necks, stuffing spilling into the flowerbeds below. The only things of beauty in this teetering pile of crap were a few toy horses and the mischievous spirit of glee with which the tower was erected.

Boros lived in his birthplace tenement around the corner from the garden for most of his 74 years. His enduring proximity, in his mind, gave him rights to a larger section of garden; so when the garden's founders restricted him to a 4-by-8-foot plot, Boros rebelled. He started with a ten-foot-high tower on his plot in the early 1980s. By the late '90s, it had reached 65-feet high and covered six garden plots. Some gardeners viciously fought the tower in vain, while others embraced its ugly charm.

Boros could often be found in a corner of the garden, carving and watching for reactions to his self-styled masterpiece. Sometimes he monkey-climbed his way to the top, where he would alert the world to his existence by honking on a French horn. An admitted drunk, Boros was known for challenging other local bar patrons to arm-wrestling. Boros died in spring 2007, after having both legs amputated earlier that year due to health issues. One year later, the city demolished his tower.

Wigstock

**Where: Tompkins Square Park and, later, the Christopher St. Piers
b. Labor Day 1984; d. Labor Day 2001**

Way back in 1984, a gaggle of drag queens tumbled out of the Pyramid Club—then the epicenter for both drag and hardcore punk rock—and into Tompkins Square Park. Drunk and inspired, they looked to the park's stage and thought, "We should be on it." So the next year, "Lady" Bunny, the most motivated of the group, set about acquiring the necessary permits and birthed Wigstock, the world's best and perhaps only outdoor drag festival.

The humor was raunchy, the makeup heavy, and the wigs gargantuan. That first year, the extravaganza of chiffon, rhinestones, Adam's apples and hairy hands lured an audience of nearly one thousand. Within ten years, the crowd had grown to 35,000. Drag acts, including the likes of Lypsinka, John Sex and the Dueling Bankheads, parodied the standard female caricatures, from whore to housewife. Freaky Brit Leigh Bowery once birthed a full-grown woman, covered in fake blood, and then chewed through the sausage-link umbilical cord. But the "Lady" Bunny ruled the stage, with her gutter-wallowing cabaret routines. "I'm gonna drain all three of your balls—and all that jizz," she'd sing over "All that Jazz."

Wigstock drew talent from the downtown club and art scenes. The Fleshtones and artist David Wojnarowicz' band 3 Teens Kill 4 were staples for years. Wigstock always maintained its essence, delivering outrageous performance art as well as high-profile DJs and dance music performers, such as Lady Miss Kier and Ultra Nate. In 2001, Mother Nature, not corporate development, rained out Wigstock for good, leaving the organizers drowning in runny mascara and unmanageable debt. It sputtered on for a few years at the HOWL Festival, but for now, it appears the Wigstock era has ended, taking its uber-bouffants and seismic beehives with it.

Websites of Related Interest

These sites know all about weirdness too.

- *Forgottenny.com*
- *Scoutingny.com*
- *Offbeatnewyork.com*
- *Vanishingnewyork.blogspot.com*
- *Roadsideamerica.com*

Geographic Index

Greenwich Village/SoHo/Tribeca/Downtown

Lower East Side/East Village

Central/West Village

Flatiron/Gramercy

Chelsea

Midtown East

Midtown West

Roosevelt Island

Upper East Side

Upper West Side/Inwood/Washington Heights

Bronx

Brooklyn

About Allan Ishac

*Allan Ishac created the New York's 50 Best series of popular guidebooks and is the author of **New York's 50 Best Places To Take Children** and **New York's 50 Best Places To Find Peace And Quiet**. He also developed and wrote the two-time Telly Award-winning Hard Hat Harry's children's video series. Allan's work in new media includes the launch of the first dot.calm website Findpeaceandquiet.com in 2008 and the related iPhone application TranquiliCity in 2010. The Guide to Odd New York is the work of Allan's darker Gemini twin.*

About Cari Jackson

*Cari Jackson is a Yankee-born, southern-raised writer and editor. She is the author of four non-fiction children's books, including **Bugs That Build, Bugs That Destroy, Alien Invasion: How Invasive Species Become Major Menaces** and **Revolution in Computers**. She has also traveled on assignment for various magazines to surf on a reef break, fall from a flying trapeze and sample mortar-size fireworks. She and her husband, JJ Rudisill, own Funhouse Skateboards (www.funhouseskateboards.com). They live in the heart of Brooklyn with their young son, Solomon, who attended many of the adventures in this book while in utero.*

Odds...and Ends!

Pratt Steam Room
The art of ogling an engine while dodging cats.

Where: 200 Willoughby Ave., bet. Classon Ave. and Hall St.
When: By appointment only
Phone: 718-636-3694
Getting there: G to Clinton and Washington, head for the massive chimney on Pratt's campus
Fee: Free
Website: pratt.edu

There's a steam engine on the Pratt Institute campus that's been thrumming away for an astonishing 110 years. It owes its preservation and long working life to an amazing New Yorker named Conrad Milster, who has championed this enormous contraption since 1958.

If you're wondering why anyone would want to make a special visit to a steam generator, consider that an oak observation deck was built on site in the Victorian era for the express purpose of allowing the public to admire this machine. If engine ogling was good enough for your immigrant relatives, why not you?

The bright red generator—looking like some crazy product of Jules Verne's imagination—is comprised of a massive electromagnet driving an equally impressive turbine. On request, Milster will open a valve to set the flywheel spinning. The resultant whirs and pffts are audible evidence of power being generated. Brass switches are mounted on gray marble panels, and a collection of antique brass meters are on display in glass cases. It's a scene right out of the early days of the industrial revolution, complete with the smell of oil and the sound of the hissing steam. You'll be gawking like a kid within seconds.

As unofficial preservationist for Pratt, Milster has turned the plant into his personal museum of eccentricity. Employed here for more than 50 years, and Chief Engineer since 1965 (he is only the fourth person to hold that title since the power plant opened in 1887), he has designed the plant with decorative pieces appropriate to the machine's era.

The two massive chandeliers towering over the steam works came from the 1906 Singer building and the formidable steam whistle was reclaimed from the French ocean liner, Normandy. When the university library started chucking some old paintings, Milster swept them up and hung them in the plant. They include the work of Brooklyn artist Louis Loeb (his pieces also hang in the Brooklyn Museum of Art) and depict life on campus, including women in a chemistry lab in 1894.

If you're lucky—and you can stand an abundance of cats—your tour may continue at Milster's campus townhouse. Inside, antique pressure gauges connected to the plant enable him to monitor the premises from home. The man has saved hundreds of books from campus trash bins, too, including an 1812 History of Westminster Abbey, with hand-tinted prints, and Practical Philosophy, from 1795. You'll also meet his 25 cats, not counting Mr. Higgy, Momma and Prancy, who hang out at the plant.

Every New Year's Eve, Milster hooks up a half-dozen steam whistles and a steam calliope to the plant. Neighborhood folks fill the quad and at midnight, Milster sounds them off, letting locals take turns unleashing the deafening toots.

A lurching man, with massive hands, mutton chops, and flyaway hair, Milster is currently searching for an apprentice. But he has no intention of retiring. He really doesn't trust anyone else with his big red toy.

See our website for more odd stuff!
www.oddnewyork.com

Odd Notes:

Odd Notes:

Odd Notes: